Language and Literacy
for the Early Years

Sally Neaum

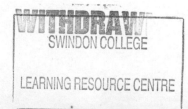

Language
and Literacy

for the Early Years

Sally Neaum

Los Angeles | London | New Delhi
Singapore | Washington DC

Learning Matters
An imprint of SAGE Publications Ltd
1 Oliver's Yard
55 City Road
London EC1Y 1SP

SAGE Publications Inc.
2455 Teller Road
Thousand Oaks, California 91320

SAGE Publications India Pvt Ltd
B 1/I 1 Mohan Cooperative Industrial Area
Mathura Road
New Delhi 110 044

SAGE Publications Asia-Pacific Pte Ltd
3 Chuch Street
#10–04 Samsung Hub
Singapore 049483

Editor: Amy Thornton
Development Editor: Geoff Barker
Production Controller: Chris Marke
Project Management: Deer Park Productions, Tavistock
Marketing Manager: Catherine Slinn
Cover Design: Wendy Scott
Typeset by: Pantek Media, Maidstone, Kent
Printed by: TJ International, Padstow, Cornwall

Library of Congress Control Number: 2012936244

British Library Cataloguing in Publication Data

A catalogue record for this book is available from the British Library.

ISBN: 978-0-85725-859-5
ISBN: 978-0-85725-741-3 (pbk)

MIX
Paper from
responsible sources
FSC
www.fsc.org   FSC® C013056

Contents

About the author

Sally Neaum is a lecturer in Early Childhood, and teaches primary English in initial teacher training. She has worked as a nursery and primary school teacher, and as an advisor in early years and inclusion. She has an M.Ed in Educational Psychology and Special Educational Needs and her doctoral research was in the pedagogy of early literacy.

Acknowledgements

The author particularly wishes to thank the following for the use of various extracts within the book: Oxford University Press for the extract from *The Kite Rider* by Geraldine McCaughrean (OUP, 2007), copyright © Geraldine McCaughrean 2001, reprinted by permission of Oxford University Press; William Nicholson and Egmont for the extract from *The Wind Singer* (2000); and Shaun Tan and Lothian Children's Books for the use of the image from *The Red Tree* (2001).

Every effort has been made to trace the copyright holders and to obtain their permission for the use of copyright material. The publisher and author will gladly receive any information enabling them to rectify any error or omission in subsequent editions.

Introduction

This book is about how children acquire language and become literate. It enables you to understand how children learn language, the role of others in supporting this learning, and how a child becomes a reader and writer. The book outlines our theoretical and research-based understandings of these processes. Learning language and becoming literate are shown to be social, interactive processes. Therefore, the vital role of others in supporting children's learning is emphasised throughout the book.

This book is divided into three sections:

- language acquisition;

- supporting children's language acquisition and development;

- becoming a reader and a writer.

Part 1: Language acquisition

Chapter 1 – An introduction to language acquisition

This chapter considers the importance of language learning. It considers how language enables us to communicate, to think, and to enter the experiences and worlds of other people. It shows how our current understandings of how children learn language have been patterned over time, and includes critiques of these different understandings. This provides a context for understanding the pedagogical practices that support children's language learning in the early years.

Chapter 2 – Understanding language acquisition and development: theories and approaches

This chapter considers how we learn to speak. It explains different theories that seek to explain language learning. The chapter concludes that our understanding of children's language learning is not definitive but is characterised by the interplay of an innate capacity to acquire language and social interaction.

Chapter 3 – Language development charts

This chapter outlines the stages of language development and identifies a range of important underpinning principles that need to inform developmental assessment in the early years. Criticisms of developmentalism are outlined, including questions about underpinning assumptions and how these may impact upon assessments made. A principled and reflexive approach to assessing children's language learning is identified as the way in which assessments can be made relevant and useful to individual children.

Chapter 4 – Talking with babies

The importance of talking to babies is outlined in this chapter. The chapter emphasises that language is learned in the context of social relationships and that early childhood has been identified as a 'sensitive' time to learn to talk. A number of factors that are important in babies and very young children's language acquisition are explained. Positive strategies for communicating with babies are outlined.

Chapter 5 – Factors that affect children's language acquisition and development

This chapter draws on our understanding of language acquisition as a combination of genetic sensitivity to language and social interaction. It explores the impact on language acquisition when either of these factors is affected. Additionally, the issue of the impact of television on children's language development is explored. Questions are raised about our current expectations of children's language learning through international comparisons of expectations of children in the early years.

Chapter 6 – Responding to children with speech, language and communication needs

This chapter identifies some of the reasons why some children have speech, language and communication needs and the impact that this can have on their social interaction, and on their learning. Early identification and intervention is recognised as important in working with these children. How to respond to children with these needs is outlined, in particular the importance of early years practitioners being skilled in their interactions with young children. The significance of observation-based assessment is explained and the importance of involving children's families in responding to the child's needs emphasised.

Part 2: Supporting children's language acquisition and development

Chapter 7 – Interaction to support language acquisition and development

This chapter considers why it is important for practitioners to know how to interact effectively with young children, and outlines ways to achieve this in practice.

Chapter 8 – Supporting bilingual and multilingual children's language learning

This chapter outlines what is meant by bilingualism and multilingualism and identifies the different patterns of language knowledge and learning that young children in settings may have. The range of benefits of being bilingual or multilingual is identified. The importance of valuing a child's home language is emphasised as an issue of rights, identity and good practice. Observable stages in learning English as an additional language are identified and strategies to support bilingual and multilingual children's language learning outlined.

Chapter 9 – Starting from the child

This chapter discusses the importance of using what a child knows, can do, and is interested in as the starting point for provision and interaction in settings. Observation is identified as the best way to establish children's current level of learning and their interests. The use of children's popular culture is highlighted as one way of achieving provision that starts from the child.

Chapter 10 – Rhymes, poems, songs, music and stories

This chapter outlines why rhymes, poems, songs, music and stories are important for children. It emphasises that they have value in themselves as activities that enrich our lives. In addition to this they support children's learning, including their language acquisition and development. The chapter discusses both the benefits of engagement with words and music and pedagogical practices to achieve this in the early years.

Chapter 11 – Creating a literate environment

This chapter explains what is meant by a literate environment and identifies ways of creating a literate environment in settings. It outlines the benefits of a literate environment in enabling children to become readers and writers.

Part 3: Becoming a reader and a writer

Chapter 12 – Understanding literacy

Being literate is a vital skill. We live in a literate world that places high value on reading and writing and so we all need to learn to read and write. This chapter enables you to understand how early literacy underpins later, conventional literacy. Metaphors are used to explain the relationship between early literacy and conventional literacy. The process of becoming literate in the early years is identified as emergent reading and writing.

Chapter 13 – Emergent literacy

Emergent reading and writing are defined in this chapter. The chapter describes ways in which children develop early reading and writing knowledge, skill, aptitude and interest. It also identifies pedagogical strategies to support the modelling of reading and writing, and the teaching of letter formation and letter sounds during play-based activities.

Chapter 14 – Phonics in the early years

English is an alphabetic writing system and so learning to read and write requires knowledge of that system. Phonics is discussed as a way to teach this alphabetic code. The current system for teaching phonics in schools is described and tensions and debates around this are discussed. Phonics teaching within early literacy is considered in a section entitled, 'What comes before phonics?'

Part 1

Language acquisition

1 An introduction to language acquisition

This chapter enables you to understand:

- why the acquisition and development of language is important;
- ways in which we understand children's language acquisition, as both a positivist development theory and a socio-cultural process.

The importance of language acquisition

Language acquisition and development refers to learning spoken language. Within the first few years of life human beings move from being only able to cry and make involuntary sounds to being able to communicate with others using a complex language system. This ability to acquire and use language is vital to our participation in society. Language can be spoken, heard, read, written or signed. Language enables us to communicate with others and it enables us to think and learn.

Spoken language enables us to form and maintain relationships with other people and to participate in the social world. It is what we use to engage with others in all spheres of life.

Spoken language is the precursor to literacy skills. In our highly literate society children need to become literate; that is to read and write. Literacy enables full participation in society. It enables us to communicate with others in a variety of different ways across time and space.

Language is also the pre-eminent tool for thinking. It is a sophisticated and flexible way to take in information and to process and store all that we know. Language enables us to hold and manipulate knowledge and concepts beyond our direct experiences and so be flexible and creative in how we use and develop knowledge.

ACTIVITY 1

As you work through this activity try to observe your thought processes.

1. *Think of a book, a cup, a ball.*
    How did you recall these things? What was 'in your head'? An image? A word?

2. *Think of home, friendship, beauty.*
    How did you recall these things? An image? Words?

continued

3. *Think of justice, love, equality.*
    How did you recall these things? How important was language to your recall of these concepts?

- *Look carefully at the three tasks above. Notice how important language is in understanding, processing and storing some concepts.*

- *What does this tell you about the importance of language acquisition and development?*

Language also enables us to go beyond our own experiences. Through language we can enter the experiences of others; language as talk and discussion, as stories, poems and plays and as commentary, gives us access to the thoughts, feelings and perceptions of other people across time and space. Language also allows us to create and communicate imagined people, places and worlds.

ACTIVITY 2

Read the following extracts. Notice how, through words, you can enter into places beyond your experience, enter into other people's thoughts and perceptions and visualise imagined worlds.

THE KITE RIDER

Further along the harbour wall, a great commotion started up, as a ship, newly arrived from the South, disembarked its passengers: a travelling circus. For the first time in his life, Haoyou saw elephants, ponderously picking their way across the gangplank, while tumblers somersaulted off the ship's rail and onto the dockside. There were acrobats in jade-green, close-fitting costumes, twirling banners of green and red, and jugglers and stilt-walkers, and a man laden from head to foot with noisy bird cages.

McCaughrean, G (2007)

CLOTHS OF HEAVEN

Had I the heavens' embroidered cloths,
Enwrought with golden and silver light,
The blue and the dim and the dark cloths
Of night and light and the half-light,
I would spread the cloths under your feet:
But I, being poor, have only my dreams;
I have spread my dreams under your feet;
Tread softly because you tread on my dreams.

Yeats, WB (1899/2009)

THE WIND SINGER

Inside there was a wide open space, completely full of muddy babies. There were tiny ones lying on mats and crawling ones scurrying about like small dogs, and toddling

continued

ones toppling into each other, and wailing ones, and ones that ran about yelling at the top of their voices. They were all completely naked, though of course also completely coated in mud. And they seemed to be having the time of their lives. They were forever colliding and trampling on each other in the most chaotic way, but somehow none of them ever came to any harm, or even made much complaint. They just bounced up again and got on with their infant concerns. In the midst of this writhing mass of babies there sat a number of very fat old ladies. Unlike the children they remained motionless, like mountain islands in a seething sea.

Nicholson, W (2000)

Language and thinking

The relationship between language and thinking is one articulated by a number of theorists. However, while theorists may agree with the fundamental point that there is a link between language and thought, they differ in their understanding of the nature and direction of this relationship.

The Sapir-Whorf hypothesis suggests that the language that we speak dominates and shapes our perception of reality. The words that we have to articulate the knowledge and concepts within a society determine what it is possible to know and understand within a given society. This is referred to as *linguistic determinism:* it assumes that language determines thinking.

In contrast, Piaget articulates a relationship in which thought exists before language and it is thought that provides the structure for language. Piaget argues that activity creates mental structures, known as schemas, and it is this cognitive structure that makes language possible and necessary. So, for Piaget, thought in its earliest stages, determines language.

Vygotsky also considered the relationship between language and thought. He theorised that thought and language are powerful but independent elements in young children's development. He proposed that thought and language had different routes; the earliest thinking is action based, for example reaching for toys or posting shapes, and the earliest language is sounds that have the function of maintaining the attention of others but are not speech, for example coos, gurgles, giggles and cries. When this pre-verbal thought and pre-cognitive speech have reached a certain level of development they come together to form verbal thinking. This occurs at approximately two years of age (Whitehead, 2010). When young children's thoughts can be verbalised it is evident in their development as egocentric speech. Vygotsky proposed that children's egocentric speech (talking out loud to themselves about the processes that they are engaged in) is self directing; it is literally thinking out loud. He theorised that this talking through what they are doing as they engage in activities enables children to plan, order and organise their thinking and eventually this speech is internalised and becomes what we know as thinking: silent internal contemplation.

Learning language

Babies and young children have to acquire language; they have to learn and develop their language skill, first in the form of listening and speaking (or signing) then later reading and writing. David Crystal (1997) describes language acquisition as 'Climbing the Language Mountain'. He observes that in order to produce speech and communicate with others, a young child speaking English will need to combine phonemes into syllables, syllables into phrases, clauses, sentences and dialogue, and construct this according to the grammatical rules that govern the English language. They will need a wide range of vocabulary and be aware of its appropriate usage. They will have to have knowledge of appropriate pitch, loudness, speed and tone of voice (prosody) and the social rules that govern conversation. Children who are growing up bilingual or multilingual will need to acquire this range of knowledge and skill for each of the languages spoken. Despite the seeming complexity of this process most children, by the time they enter school, will have a good grasp of the language, or languages, that they have been exposed to within their community. They will be able to use language for a variety of purposes, employing a range of vocabulary and with a high level of grammatical correctness. This acquisition of spoken language will have taken place with apparent ease, with very little direct instruction and in a relatively short period of time. How does this happen?

DEFINITION

Grammar: the rules governing the use of a language.

Understanding language learning within child development

Our understanding of how children learn language is part of wider understandings about children and childhood. From the eighteenth century onwards there were profound political, economic, technological, social and cultural changes in societies throughout Europe. Societies were changing from predominantly rural, agricultural-based societies to ones based on industrial capitalism. The move was strongly influenced by advances in science and technology. These advances precipitated a strong belief in the power of the scientific and technological as a way to understand and control the world, including an aspiration to understand and mould our own species: human beings. Within this context, encouraged by the work of Charles Darwin, emerged the Child Study Movement. The aim was to highlight the role of the biological processes in human development. The approach was scientific: the belief in, and use of, testing, observation and experimentation to discover universal laws expressed as theory. The movement demonstrated, and popularised, the view that children's conception and mental processes differed from those of adults. The development of children, therefore, became an area for scientific study and understanding, the outcomes of which, it was hoped, would identify focused interventions that would shape and mould children's lives.

Paediatric medicine and the child psychology movement

Prout (2005) identifies two important disciplines that strongly influenced the Child Study Movement and focused attention on biological aspects of being a child: the development of the science of paediatric medicine and the child psychology movement.

Paediatric medicine

The development of the discipline of paediatric medicine was an important part of the rise of the scientific study of children. The understanding of childhood disease as a separate branch of medicine became formalised in 1901 by the foundation of the Society for the Study of Diseases of Children. A medical model of children and childhood, in which children's development can be measured, monitored and managed, thus became part of how children's development, including language learning, was understood.

Child psychology

Alongside paediatrics a discipline emerging from the Child Study Movement was the development of child psychology. Prout (2005) argues that there were multiple strands of research and investigation that came together to support the understanding of children and their development, namely the work of Skinner on behaviourism, Bowlby's work on attachment, Freud and psychoanalysis, the work of Piaget and the cognitive psychology movement, and an emerging understanding of language development.

These psychological understandings came together to create a discipline of child psychology. In this emerging discipline, children were examined and tested in order to identify 'normal' ranges of functioning and behaviour that were defined and named. These assertions of what constitutes normal functioning also created the potential for defining abnormal and pathological behaviour (Prout, 2005). This 'abnormal' functioning became the site for intervention and a range of professions developed around identifying children who would benefit from intervention. Language development was one of the many aspects of children's development which professionals sought to understand, assess and in which to intervene. These psychological frameworks for understanding child development quickly became part of a general understanding of children and childhood. The language of psychology such as 'stages of development', 'attachment' and 'bonding' entered everyday talk and practice (Prout, 2005). At this stage in its development child psychology was predominantly informed by a biological view of child development; children and childhood were viewed as universal constants. The approach was to think about the individual child without consideration of the context of their social world. Within this discipline, development, whether typical or atypical, was regarded as a 'within-child' phenomenon and explanations sought through theories developed within a scientific and/or medical framework. This approach can be referred to as positivist developmental.

The emergence of a social model of childhood

Towards the end of the twentieth century there was growing criticism of how child psychology conceptualised childhood (Prout, 2005). The concern centred on an increasing awareness of, and sensitivity to, the social context of children's development. Prout observes that *at the centre of this critical approach was the notion that children are shaped by their different social contexts and that this cannot be left out of the psychological account* (2005:51).

He cites the work of Bronfenbrenner and Vygotsky as having particular importance in the emergence of a social model of childhood. Their work, and that of others, moved the debate about children's development away from the emphasis on child development purely as an inevitable biological unfolding towards an understanding that development occurs through the interplay of biology and social experience.

Urie Bronfenbrenner (1917–2005)

Bronfenbrenner developed a model that focused on the importance of both biological factors and the social environment in children's development. He proposed that while a child's biological development unfolds there is also a complex pattern of interaction with people and social patterns, institutions, and the environment around the child that similarly influences child development. Bronfenbrenner's work began to reframe the understanding of children, away from the ideas that children and childhood are universal constants that can be observed and defined in a scientific model and towards a more complex view of children and childhood. This view recognised that childhood was experienced differently by different children in different societies. So, while it could be observed that many biological factors remained similar across different societies, differences in children and the experience of childhood were due to their social experiences.

ACTIVITY 3

A baby in the first two years of life will learn to talk. How do you think this happens? Read the statements below. Which ones do you think explain why and how children learn to talk? Give reasons for you answers.

- *Babies make sounds that are like words – and the positive response from adults and older children encourages them to continue making these sounds/words and so learn to speak.*

- *Babies have a sensitivity to language which combines with a child's experiences to enable them to acquire language.*

- *Learning to talk is genetically programmed.*

- *Babies have an internal drive to communicate and learn by mimicking language and communicative behaviours from the community in which they grow and learn.*

- *Babies have no inherent ability to acquire language so their learning will depend entirely on their experiences after they are born.*

Read the next section on understanding language acquisition and then return to these statements. How has your understanding of how children learn to talk changed?

These changing ways in which we understand children and their development are reflected in our current understandings of language learning. In early years, language learning is understood within positivist developmental theory and a socio-cultural approach. Language acquisition understood within positivist developmental theory has a structural orientation. It focuses on the mental structures, processes and patterns in language learning. A socio-cultural approach to understanding language learning is orientated towards the communicative functions of language: the ways in which we acquire and use language within social and cultural practices in the society in which we grow and learn.

It is important to understand that no single approach is currently accepted as 'the truth'. Each represents a different way of understanding young children's language learning which together inform assessment of a child's language learning. Differences tend to reflect the emphasis people place on a positivist developmental approach or a socio-cultural approach, rather than an outright rejection of other approaches.

A positivist approach to language learning

A positivist approach understands language learning as progressive and developmental. Within developmentalism there are clear expectations of patterns and rates of development which are linked to norms and measures. Development, including language learning, is understood as an individual developmental process.

Checklist for Making Sounds

NHS

Screening Programmes

Newborn Hearing

4 months – a baby:
Makes soft sounds when awake. Gurgles and coos.

6 months – a baby:
Makes laughter-like sounds. Starts to make sing-song vowel sounds,
e.g. a-a, muh, goo, der, aroo, adah.

9 months – a baby:
Makes sounds to communicate in friendliness or annoyance. Babbles (e.g. 'da da da', 'ma ma ma', 'ba ba ba'). Shows pleasure in babbling loudly and tunefully. Starts to imitate other sounds like coughing or smacking lips.

12 months – a baby:
Babbles loudly, often in a conversational-type rhythm. May start to use one or two recognisable words.

15 months – a baby:
Makes lots of speech-like sounds. Uses 2-6 recognisable words meaningfully (e.g. 'teddy' when seeing or wanting the teddy bear).

18 months – a baby:
Makes speech-like sounds with conversational-type rhythm when playing. Uses 6-20 recognisable words. Tries to join in nursery rhymes and songs.

24 months – a child:
Uses 50 or more recognisable words appropriately. Puts 2 or more words together to make simple sentences e.g. more milk. Joins in nursery rhymes and songs. Talks to self during play (may be incomprehensible to others).

30 months – a child:
Uses 200 or more recognisable words. Uses pronouns (e.g. I, me, you). Uses sentences but many will lack adult structure. Talks intelligibly to self during play. Asks questions. Says a few nursery rhymes.

36 months – a child:
Has a large vocabulary intelligible to everyone.

Adapted from: M. D. Sheridan (Revised by M. Frost and A. Sharma), 1997, Routledge, London, New York.

Figure 1.1: Child development chart: My Personal Child Health Record (NHS)

Critiques of positivist development theory

Positivist language development theory has been criticised for a number of reasons. As outlined above, developmentalism arose from a tradition that sought to understand, classify and intervene in human development. In achieving this, developmentalism sought to measure and create norms for children's development. However, as critics observe, any system that creates norms also creates the potential for 'not normal'. This is often linked to the expectation that there will be an intervention to normalise development (Burman, 2008). The assumption of developmental norms in language learning is strongly criticised because assessment of a child's development in this way is decontexualised: it fails to take account of individual children's linguistic and cultural heritage as well as their language learning experiences. Language learning is, critics argue, a socially-embedded learning process and so any analysis of a child's ability must take this into account. As Burman comments, we must study the context as well as the child.

THEORY FOCUS

Ways with words

Shirley Brice Heath conducted an ethnographical study (1983) over nine years in which she worked, lived and played in two different communities in the American south in order to develop an understanding of how the children in the communities learned to use language. She called these two communities Roadville and Trackton.

She concluded that the different ways in which the children learned to use language were dependent on the ways in which each community structured their families, defined the roles of community members and played out their concepts of childhood that guided the socialisation of their children. Children in Roadville and Trackton came to have different ways of communicating, because their communities had different legacies and ways of behaving in face-to-face interactions.

Brice Heath found that the children in Trackton learned language by telling stories, making metaphors and seeing patterns across items and events, and this did not fit with the accepted developmental patterns of linguistic or cognitive growth. In contrast, the children in Roadville seemed to have had experiences that enabled them to develop many of the linguistic patterns equated with readiness for school.

A socio-cultural understanding of language acquisition

This approach focuses on the social aspects of acquiring language. It seeks to understand the contextualised process of language learning through social interaction. Social-cultural theory explores how our social and cultural context shapes our knowledge and experience of language learning. It focuses on the social aspects of language learning rather than the individual. The underlying assumption is that a child's language will reflect their social and cultural experiences. This understanding of language learning is exemplified in Brice Heath's (1903) work above.

Critiques of a socio-cultural approach to understanding language acquisition

Critiques of a socio-cultural approach are pragmatic. A purely socio-cultural approach tends to be relativist rather than definitive so development is regarded as contextualised and therefore idiosyncratic. This does not enable easy comparative assessments of development to be made. At a pragmatic level, developmental norms provide benchmarks for assessments to be made. Within the current health, education and social care systems, definitive developmental assessments are often the way to access additional support. Within language learning, where there are decisions to be made about interventions or access to funding or support, normative developmental charts enable comparative assessments of children's abilities and needs. Therefore, in a practical way, developmental norms are a useful working tool for many people working with young children.

Combining the approaches: complementary or judgemental?

A positivist developmental approach and a socio-cultural approach to understanding children's language acquisition and development are not necessarily mutually exclusive. Indeed they can be complementary, offering a holistic view of a young child's language learning. At best, we may, for example, assess children's language ability against normative development charts and take account of their social and cultural language learning experiences to enable a more nuanced description of their ability and needs. However, there is also the potential to be judgemental, for example, measuring children's language learning against normative development charts and then using their cultural and social language learning experiences to explain any perceived deficit in their language ability and to label and blame individuals and communities for not being 'good enough'.

Conclusion

Our current understanding of language learning is not definitive. We do not yet fully understand how children learn to talk. However, developmentalism and a socio-cultural approach offer a broad framework for understanding stages in children's language development, and the impact of the child's experiences within their family and community, both of which are observable in young children's language acquisition and learning.

SUMMARY

In this chapter we have considered the importance of language learning. We have seen how language enables us to communicate and to think and how it enables us to enter the experiences of other people and other worlds, both real and imagined. We have seen how current understandings of children have been patterned over time. Two different approaches to understanding language learning have been explained: a positivist developmental approach and a socio-cultural approach. These different approaches are exemplified in an example from My Personal Child Health Record *(NHS) and the work of Shirley Brice Heath (1983). The question of how these approaches are used in early years provision has been explored.*

FURTHER READING

Brice Heath, S (1983) *Ways with Words. Language, Life and Work in Communities and Classrooms.* New York: Cambridge University Press.

Burman, E (2008) *Deconstructing Developmental Psychology.* London: Routledge.

Crystal, D (1998) *Language Play.* London: Penguin.

Dahlberg, G, Moss, P and Pence, P (1999) *Beyond Quality in Early Childhood and Care. Postmodern Perspectives.* London: Falmer Books.

Guldberg, H (2009) *Reclaiming Childhood. Freedom and Play in an Age of Fear.* London: Routledge.

James, A and Prout, A (1997) *Constructing and Reconstructing Childhood. Contemporary Issues in the Sociological Study of Childhood.* London: RoutledgeFalmer.

Layard, R and Dunn, J (2009) *A Good Childhood. Searching for Values in a Competitive Age.* London: Penguin.

Moss, P and Petrie, P (2002) *From Children's Services to Children's Spaces: Public Policy, Children and Childhood.* London: RoutledgeFalmer.

Prout, A (2005) *The Future of Childhood.* Abingdon: RoutledgeFalmer.

Pugh, G and Duffy, B (2006) *Contemporary issues in the Early Years.* London: SAGE.

Wells, G (1987) *The Meaning Makers: Children Learning Language and Using Language to Learn.* London: Hodder and Stoughton Educational.

2 Understanding language acquisition and development: theories and approaches

This chapter enables you to understand:

- the different theoretical perspectives on how language is acquired and developed: behaviourism; nativism (linguistic approach); social interactionism; usage-based model.

Introduction

Have you ever thought about how you learned to speak and communicate with other people? Who supported this learning? How did they support it? What would you do to support a young child's language acquisition? Why would you do this? What does this tell you about what you understand about how children acquire language? Where is your understanding from? What ideas underpin your understanding of young children's language learning? This chapter aims to answer some of these questions. It explores different theories that support our current understanding of young children's language acquisition.

Changing understandings of language learning

Alongside all other understandings of children and their development there have been changing views on how children learn language. In line with other understandings of children's development (outlined in Chapter 1) language learning has been explained in different ways. Different theories and explanations have, in their time, attempted to answer emerging questions about how young children learn language. The theories tend to reflect the wider context in which they were developed. They are perhaps best understood as a developing story: a story that we, as yet, do not fully comprehend, a story in which each theory or explanation contributes to our current understanding of young children's language learning.

Behaviourism

A behaviourist explanation of language acquisition applies the principles of reinforcement to language learning. Language learning is understood in the same way as all other learned behaviours: a process of stimulus and response. In this theory language is learned and shaped through external reinforcement. It is understood as small steps towards speaking encouraged through responses from other people. For example, a child babbles 'mamamama' and the response from parents and other adults assumes that this is an attempt at saying 'mummy', and they demonstrate their delight at this. This delight acts as positive reinforcement which encourages the child to repeat that sound and to engage in the dynamic of making sounds and receiving positive feedback. The child is seen as relatively passive in this process in that other people determine what the child learns through reinforcing the behaviours that they wish to continue.

A behaviourist understanding of language learning was, in its time, in line with other explanations of how humans learn. It emerged as part of the behaviourist school of psychology through the work of theorists such as Pavlov, Watson, Thorndike and Skinner. Their work was predominantly experimental laboratory work with a focus on how animals and humans *behave* rather than how they think or feel. In their experiments they showed that they were able to influence behaviour by linking a stimulus to a response. A behaviourist approach understands language learning in the same way: children produce 'language behaviours', other people respond, and this creates a stimulus-response dynamic which moulds and shapes the child's language.

ACTIVITY **1**

Read these sentences.

* *I goed to the shop.*

* *I drinked my drink.*

* *I saw three mouses.*

In each of these sentences are words that young children are very unlikely to have heard but occur in their speech. What are the implications for a behaviourist explanation of language acquisition?

Critics suggest that behaviourism has limitations in fully explaining how children learn, and learn to use, our complex language system. Knowledge of young children's speech suggests that language learning goes beyond basic reinforcement of utterances. There are a number of reasons for this.

* The volume of language that we need to enable us to communicate and learn is vast; it would be impossible to reinforce this for each individual utterance for each child.

* We create and use innovative and, at times, unique language which hasn't been reinforced.

* Children use words incorrectly that they don't hear and aren't reinforced (see Activity 1 above).

Behaviourism is therefore unlikely to fully explain how we learn language although, as Whitehead (2010) suggests, it may have some part to play in the initial stages of language acquisition and later on in learning and extending vocabulary and in developing phonology and phonetics.

THEORY FOCUS

Behaviourists

JB Watson (1878–1958)

Watson was one of the earliest and most 'extreme' behaviourists. He argued that everything from speech to emotional responses were simply patterns of stimulus and response. He called this conditioning. He denied the existence of the mind or consciousness. Learning began as trial and error and the conditioned behaviour was formed through feedback about what worked and what didn't work. He concluded that the stimulus-response bond was formed though feedback which moulded the response. Watson and Raynor (1920) conducted a famous (and now ethically questionable) experiment on 'little Albert' to demonstrate how classical conditioning, outlined by Pavlov, could be applied to humans to create a phobia. This demonstrated the learned link that is made between stimuli and response.

'Little Albert' was nine months old. In the experiment he was shown a toy white rat, a rabbit, a monkey and some masks (stimuli). He showed no fear of these stimuli. However, he was frightened when a hammer was struck against a steel bar behind his head. The sudden loud noise caused him to burst into tears. Watson demonstrated that he could create a learned link between the stimuli and response.

At eleven months old the white rat was presented and seconds later the hammer was struck against the steel bar. This was done several times over the next weeks and each time he burst into tears. Eventually, 'little Albert' only had to see the rat and he immediately showed every sign of fear. He would cry and he attempted to crawl away even when there was no accompanying sudden loud sound. He had learned the link between the stimulus and his response. Over the following weeks his response lessened but remained evident. Watson called this 'extinction'.

Classical conditioning is therefore the active eliciting of a response through the use of a particular stimulus.

EL Thorndike (1874–1949)

Thorndike was working at the same time as Watson. He too was interested in how behaviourist techniques can be applied to human behaviour. He was particularly interested in the effects of different types of response. Thorndike concluded that satisfying and gratifying responses were more effective in establishing behaviours. This conclusion was, and remains, influential in learning theory: that positive reinforcement, rather than punishment, is more effective in promoting learning behaviours.

BF Skinner (1904–1990)

Skinner is probably the best known of the behaviourist theorists. He further developed the idea of conditioning. Skinner described what he called *operant conditioning*. In operant conditioning desired responses are reinforced. A person acts (operates) and this elicits the

continued

THEORY FOCUS continued

reinforcement. The person reinforcing the behaviour waits until the required behaviour is emitted then acts to reinforce that behaviour. Skinner drew a number of conclusions about learning from his experiments. These include:

- steps in learning should be small and linked to previous learning;

- reinforcement should be frequent in the early stages of learning and then can become more intermittent as learning progresses.

Nativism

ACTIVITY 2

Record a friend describing what you are wearing. Transcribe the recording (write down exactly what was said).

Analyse the transcript. Can you spot the following?

- *mms and errs;*

- *colloquial (local 'slang') words;*

- *fillers – 'like', 'sort-of', 'kind-of';*

- *unfinished sentences;*

- *sentences that change direction part way through;*

- *indistinct words or mumbling.*

As you will have discovered, our spoken language is not precise, correct and beautifully formed! This is predominantly what children hear as they learn to speak. We do tend to slow our speech down and be more precise and focused when we speak directly to very young children but this approach diminishes as children acquire language.

What does this suggest about how children acquire language?

The nativist view of language acquisition emerged, in part, from interest in the question, 'How do we acquire language that we are not directly taught?' Nativists argued that even the most straightforward observation and analysis of children's language shows that they learn and use complex language structures with only limited direct instruction and reinforcement, and from exposure to rather imprecise language use from the people around them. Additionally, language acquisition is universal; all people, without specific language learning problems, learn to speak. They concluded that the behaviourist explanation of language acquisition was too simplistic to explain the complexity and universality of language acquisition.

Chomsky and Universal Grammar

One of the most influential people in developing and articulating a nativist view of language development was Noam Chomsky. Chomsky's work focused on the structures of the mind that enable us to learn language. He was interested in understanding how young children process the language that they hear. Chomsky proposed the idea of a 'Universal Grammar'. He argued that certain aspects of our knowledge and understanding, including language, are genetically determined. Universal Grammar is one such potential that we are born with and that develops over time through genetic unfolding. Chomsky argues that we are all born with the same potential to acquire language and this develops into knowledge of the particular language, or languages, to which we are exposed. This internal potential that makes language learning possible is referred to as a 'Language Acquisition Device (LAD)'. This LAD enables us to abstract the governing rules of the language, or languages, that we hear (or see) and to generate utterances in that language (Smidt, 2011). Language learning is thus essentially an autonomous, internal, individual process. It is a process in which language acquisition is understood as being built from grammatical rules into communication. This LAD, Chomsky argued, offers an explanation for how children acquire complex language systems and for the universality of language acquisition.

Similarly to the behaviourists, the work of Chomsky and other nativists advanced the understanding of language learning but left some important questions unanswered. Chomsky has been criticised for an over-emphasis on grammar and structure in language rather than meaning. Critics argue that the most important function of language is to create meaning in a social world; that language acquisition is essentially a social, communicative process rather than an internal, structural, purely linguistic process. Therefore, Chomsky, in focusing on structure and disregarding the importance of meaning, fails to take account of the most important aspect of language learning; that it is a social process in a social world.

A growing focus on social aspects of learning was part of a wider movement in psychology influenced by the work of Urie Bronfenbrenner (see page 12). Bronfenbrenner proposed that children's experiences in the social world in which they lived were highly significant in their learning and development. His *The Ecology of Human Development* (1979) demonstrated the significance of immediate and wider social environments on learning, and, although he didn't focus specifically on language development, his theory regarding the impact of social experiences on learning was significant in the developing emphasis on social interaction in learning.

Social interaction and language learning

The work of Lev Vygotsky and Jerome Bruner was influential in addressing the issue of an over-emphasis on structure and grammar and developing our current understanding of the significance of social interaction in language learning. They revealed the intense social nature of language acquisition, starting from a baby's seemingly innate drive to communicate with others.

This focus on social interaction doesn't preclude the possibility of genetic inheritance but emphasises a different function and aspect of language learning. Language learning from this perspective is understood as communication driven and socially shaped; that is, the drive to acquire language is to enable us to communicate with others, and how we know, use and develop language is dependent upon our experiences in the social world.

ACTIVITY 3

The social context of language learning

Recall being with a family or group of people who you didn't grow up with, for example a friend or partner's family or colleagues at work. Can you recall the ways in which they interacted that were different to your own family and/or community? For example:

- *Ways of addressing each other, for example: where I currently live, wives/partners are sometimes referred to as 'our lass'.*

- *Tone and patterns of interaction, for example: is it jovial, formal, teasing, relaxed, tense? Who is 'in charge'? Who contributes? Who is quiet?*

- *The subjects that people choose to talk about and the subjects that are unacceptable.*

- *Qualitative aspects of language that are used to communicate.*

- *The 'in' jokes, jests and teases.*

- *Words and/or ways of interacting that are very particular to the family or group and that an outsider would find difficult to access immediately.*

- *Words that are regional or colloquial.*

- *Words or ways of interacting that clash with expectations within your own family or community.*

Why do you think that these aspects of interaction are different in different families and communities? Where and how do people learn these ways of being? What does this indicate about the social nature of language acquisition and development?

Lev Vygotsky

Lev Vygotsky's work, emphasised the importance of the social world in children's development. He argued that it is through others that we become ourselves. It is in our interactions with others that we create who we are, and it is the cultural tool of language that expresses this in communication, and articulates it in thought.

Vygotsky's work focused on the importance of the social context in language acquisition rather than the processes involved. The main premise of his work is that as humans we have a range of psychological tools that enable us to use and extend our mental abilities. These tools are symbolic systems that we use to interpret and communicate reality and include signs, symbols, plans, numbers, musical notation, charts, models, pictures and, above all, language (Dolya, 2010). These tools are developed in families and communities and become part of the culture which is then passed on to children as they grow and learn. For Vygotsky, language is the pre-eminent cultural tool and it is vital because of the interrelationship between thought and language. Language, he argues, forms the basis of thought. This means that the development of thought is closely linked to a child's language ability. This ability is, in turn, dependent upon the socio-cultural context in which the child is acquiring and developing their language.

ACTIVITY 4

Symbolic systems

Pick up a pen and pretend that it is:

* *an aeroplane;*

* *fork;*

* *a sword.*

Each time that you use the pen to represent something else you are demonstrating the ability to symbolise: to use one thing to represent another.

This is an important skill as language, in all its forms (spoken, read, written, signed) is a symbolic representation of our world, both what we perceive and what we think.

We use other symbolic systems, as well as language, to represent our world.

What do we use these symbolic systems to represent?

* *music notation;*

* *maps;*

* *numbers;*

* *pictures;*

* *models.*

Jerome Bruner – Language Acquisition Support System (LASS)

Jerome Bruner's significant contribution to our current understanding of language acquisition was his addition of a LASS to Chomsky's LAD. Bruner was concerned that Chomsky paid little, if any, attention to the role of interaction in language learning. Bruner's Language Acquisition Support System (LASS) aimed to address this. He argued that in order for the Language Acquisition Device (LAD – see page 21) to develop, children who are learning to speak need to be involved in clear, predictable and repeated interactions with others. This social interaction, in all its forms, is the LASS.

Bruner's work on language acquisition is part of his wider understanding that learning is an active process in which learners are engaged in constructing new ideas and concepts. This construction of ideas and concepts is supported by more knowledgeable adults who scaffold the learning in a way that is appropriate to the learner's current state of understanding. In language acquisition Bruner agrees that there must be an innate linguistic capacity that enables the child to construct the grammar, but children are able to acquire this grammar effectively because the people around them create a meaningful world of interaction. Children's daily routines, interactions and play provide the framework for this interaction in which the meaning is indicated by the context. This LASS to accompany Chomsky's LAD is, in Bruner's view, how a child acquires language.

CASE STUDY

Peek-a boo and Bruner's LASS

Imogen was lying in her cot watching her mobile. As her mummy came into the room Imogen turned her head towards the door. As she turned her head Helen, her mummy, stepped behind the door and hid from Imogen briefly before appearing again, caught Imogen's eye and, with exaggerated intonation, said, 'There you are lovely girl'.

Imogen smiled.

Helen stepped behind the door and repeated the sequence.

Imogen giggled.

Helen repeated the sequence several times each time leaving her appearance a few seconds longer to hold the suspense. Within a few repetitions Imogen was anticipating her mummy's appearance, watching intently and giggling before she appeared.

This is an example of the LASS in action. Helen uses language in a clear, repeated, meaningful and enjoyable social context. This engages with Imogen's drive to communicate with her mummy and supports her acquisition of language to enable her to do this more effectively.

Bruner observed that the game of peek-a-boo is one of the repeated patterns of interaction within most children's lives. It may start simply but can also build into quite complex ritualised games of disappearance and reappearance accompanied by, and interpreted through, language. Through these interactions the child learns: the syntax of language; words, phrases and utterances needed to play the game; how to take turns in social interaction; and how to construct a sequence of interaction so that it is meaningful and interesting.

A usage-based model of language acquisition

Tomasello (2003) further develops the idea of language acquisition as a social process in his usage-based model of language acquisition. His argument turns Chomsky's notion of a universal grammar on its head. For Tomasello, language acquisition and development flow *from* communication *to* rule-based grammar. This is in contrast to Chomsky who sees language acquisition as building *from* grammatical rules *to* communication.

Tomasello argues that language structures emerge from language use. The symbolic and representational dimensions of language occur first, as we communicate with others, and grammar is derived from these communicative utterances.

Hansen (2010) describes this succinctly.

- The linguistic (Chomskian) hypothesis is: *the small child understands words, and thereby decodes contextual meaning.*

- The usage-based hypothesis is: *the small child decodes contextual meaning, and thereby understands words.*

The basis of this patterning of language structures from communication is, in Tomasello's view, integrated with other cognitive and social-cognitive skills. He argues that these more general cognitive and social-cognitive skills enable children to pattern their communicative utterances into the structures of language, namely:

1. intention reading;

2. pattern finding.

Intention reading emerges at about nine to twelve months of age and includes things such as the ability to:

- follow the attention and gestures of others;

- direct the attention of others by pointing, showing and using other non-linguistic gestures;

- *learn* the intentional gestures of others including their communicative functions.

Intention reading skills are necessary for children as they enable them to acquire the appropriate use of communicative symbols which eventually lead to the use of more complex linguistic expressions and constructions.

Pattern finding skills include the ability to:

- recognise categories of similar objects and events;

- to form sensory motor schemas.

These skills are necessary for children to find patterns in the way adults use linguistic symbols in utterances to construct the grammar of a language.

Intention reading and pattern finding are skills that enable children to construct grammatical structures through communicative interactions and utterances. This has important implications for early years practitioners as it adds significantly to our understanding regarding interaction with children pre-linguistically. A usage-based approach requires that we recognise and encourage intention-sharing and pattern-finding skills and engage with these communicative symbols as an integral part of young children's language acquisition.

Conclusion

Our understanding of how children learn to talk is not yet definitive. However, the interplay of an innate capacity to acquire language and social interaction characterises our current understanding of language acquisition and development. It underpins advice to parents and our early years setting guidance, and informs intervention strategies for children who require additional support.

SUMMARY

This chapter has asked you to consider how we learn to speak. Different theories to explain this process have been explored, including questions that remain unanswered by different theoretical perspectives. The chapter concludes that the current understanding of language learning is one that acknowledges that we have an innate capacity to acquire language but that an interactive social context is necessary for a child to learn to speak.

FURTHER READING

Saxton, M (2010) *Child Language. Acquisition and Development.* London: SAGE.

Tomasello, M (2003) *Constructing a Language. A Usage-Based Theory of Language Acquisition.* London: Harvard University Press.

Whitehead, M (2010) *Language and Literacy in the Early Years 0–7.* 4th Edition. London: SAGE.

3 Language development charts

This chapter enables you to understand:

- principles of child development;
- the pattern of language development;
- some critiques of developmentalism.

Introduction

This chapter outlines the developmental sequences that children go through as they acquire language. The charts identify expected developmental progression in language acquisition, from a baby's initial eye contact to a child being able to use language to take on a role in imaginary play. This developmental approach to understanding children's language acquisition is underpinned by a number of important principles. These principles are outlined in this chapter.

Developmental assessment, against established norms, is used throughout children's services to establish that children's growth and development is as expected and, when appropriate, to identify areas of need. However, this approach has been critiqued. This critique of a developmental approach will be explored in this chapter.

Principles of child development

Categorising and describing language acquisition in developmental charts enables us to understand and assess the pace, progress and pattern of a child's learning. Developmental charts enable assessment of children's development to be made against norms, which can, when used effectively, contribute to supporting children's language acquisition. However, these charts should not be used in isolation. Effective developmental assessment needs to take account of a set of very important principles that underpin all aspects of child development.

Children's development:

- is holistic;
- has multiple determinants;
- has a predictable sequence and direction;
- is cumulative;
- is characterised by individual variation.

Children's development is holistic

All aspects of children's learning and development are interrelated, inseparable and interdependent. Language development occurs simultaneously with all other areas of development (physical, intellectual, social and emotional) and affects them and is affected by them.

Children's development has multi-determinants

Children learn and develop through a complex interplay of biological and social factors. Their learning and development occur as a result of who they are and what they experience. The pace and progress of their development is determined both by genetic imperative and social experiences.

Children's language development occurs within the context of their lives. The context is determined by culture, community and family and is influenced by the children themselves. Children are part of the context in which they are conceived, born and develop and, because social processes are dynamic two-way processes, the context will have an impact on the child and the child will have an impact on the context in which they grow and learn to talk. Children's language development will reflect this.

Children's development has a predictable sequence and direction

The sequence of children's development usually remains predictable regardless of the pace of progress, for example in language learning, babbling comes before single words and single words before sentences.

There are, of course, exceptions to this and, as Bruce and Meggitt (2002) point out, it may be useful to see developmental patterns as similar rather than the same. They suggest that development may be viewed as a web or network of knowledge, skills and aptitudes rather than always a linear progression. This may be particularly important for children with communication and language difficulties whose acquisition and development of language may be atypical.

Children's development also tends to follow a number of directional sequences. Those associated with language acquisition and development are:

- *from simple to complex* – sounds to babbling to single words to combinations of words;

- *from general to specific* – communicating pleasure through whole body movement as a baby, to smiling, to the use of words and/or gesture.

Children's development is cumulative

Children's development begins before birth and continues after birth. Each stage of development builds on a previous stage, for example babbling is an important precursor to speech. This means that children need to go through developmental phases with sufficient time and experience at each phase to learn, and to consolidate their learning to ensure that they have a secure basis for future learning. Therefore there should be no urgency to move children through stages quickly. Careful consideration, through observation and assessment of learning, needs to be given at each stage of development to ensure children have had sufficient time and experience to learn, and to consolidate their learning, before moving on. Engaging in early communication through gesture, facial expression and vocalisation, and talking with children in their play and daily routines, will provide these opportunities for children to learn language.

Children's development is characterised by individual variation

Within any group of children there will be a variation in the pace of individual progress within and between developmental areas and there will be a variation in the comparative progress of children. This is to be expected because children's development has multiple determinants. In language development variations will occur because of the social context in which children acquire and are developing their language. Developmental charts therefore need to be understood in terms of ranges of age and developmental norms rather than fixed ages linked to stages. It is only when children fall significantly outside of these developmental parameters, or when there is a significant discrepancy between developmental areas, that there should be cause for concern.

Developmental progression

Children's language development can be observed progressing through a series of identifiable stages. The pace of progress will depend partly upon the child's chronological age, in line with maturational development of sound-producing physiology, but progress is also profoundly influenced by the context in which the child is learning language. The table below shows developmental levels from birth to five years.

Approximate age	Developmental level
Birth	• Involuntary cry.
2–3 weeks	• Signs of intentional communication: eye contact.
6 weeks onward	• Children may smile when spoken to. • Cooing and gurgling begin in response to parent or carer's presence and voice; also to show contentment.
1–2 months	• Children may move their eyes or head towards the direction of the sound. • Children begin to discriminate between consonant sounds.
3 months	• Children will raise their head when sounds attract their attention.
4–5 months	• Playful sounds appear; most are in response to the human voice and to show contentment. • Cooing and laughing appear. • Children respond to familiar sounds by turning their head, kicking or stopping crying. • Child may shout to attract attention.
6 months	• The beginning of babbling, regular repeated sounds and playing around with these sounds. This is important for practising sound-producing mechanisms necessary for later speech. • Babbling is 'reduplicated babbling' at this stage – consonants (C) and vowels (V) together in repeated CV syllables – ba ba ba ba ba. • Cooing, laughing and gurgling become stronger. • Children begin to understand emotion in the parent or carer's voice. • Children begin to enjoy music and rhymes, particularly if accompanied by actions and animated facial expression.

continued

9 months	• Babbling continues and the repertoire increases. • Babbling is now 'variegated' – children produce strings of different sounds – ba-ma. • Babbling takes on the stresses and intonation of the language (or languages) that the child is hearing. • Children begin to recognise their own name. • The range of vowel sounds produced start to resemble the language that the child is hearing – they are 'tuning' in to the language(s) around them. • May understand simple, single words such as 'No' or 'Bye-Bye'. • Children continue to enjoy music and rhymes and will now attempt to join in with the actions, e.g. Pat-a-cake.
9–12 months	• Babbling reflects the intonation of speech. • Consonants begin to reflect the language(s) that the child is hearing. • Children may imitate simple words. This is usually an extension of babbling, e.g. dada. • Pointing begins. This is often accompanied by a sound or the beginnings of a word. This demonstrates an increasing awareness that words are associated with people, objects and actions.
12 months	• Children's vocabulary starts to develop but may remain quite limited as children concentrate on achieving mobility. • Passive vocabulary (words that the child understands but doesn't yet say) increases rapidly. • Pointing accompanied by a single word is the basis of verbal communication.
15 months	• Children's active vocabulary (words that the child can say and use appropriately) increases: this tends to be names of familiar things and people. • Children use their language(s) to name belongings and point out named objects. • Children overextend words, e.g. 'dog' for all furry animals with four legs. • Less frequently they underextend words, e.g. 'cat' only for their cat not the one next door. • One word and intonation is used to indicate meaning, e.g. 'cup' may mean 'I want a drink' or 'I have lost my cup' etc. The intonation and possibly the situation would indicate the meaning to people who are familiar with the child. This is called the holophrasic stage. • Children will repeat words or sentences.
21 months	• Both passive and active vocabularies rapidly increase (the passive vocabulary remains larger than the active). • Children begin to name objects and people that are not there; this shows the development of language for thinking. • Sentences begin, initially as two-word phrases, e.g. 'Mummy gone'. • Gesture is still a fundamental part of communication. • Children begin asking questions usually, 'What?', 'Who?' etc.
2 years	• Both active and passive vocabularies continue to increase. • Children can generalise words but this sometimes means they over-generalise, e.g. all men are 'daddy'. • Personal pronouns (words instead of actual names) are used, e.g. he, she, etc. They are not always used correctly. • Sentences become longer although they tend to be in telegraphic speech, i.e. only the main sense-conveying words are used like 'Mummy gone work'. • Questions are asked frequently, 'What?' 'Why?'. • The plural form of words is often over generalised; children may refer to mouses or sheeps. • Irregular verb forms may be used, i.e. seed (for saw) and comed (for came). • In speech final consonants and unstressed syllables are often omitted, i.e 'ca' for 'cat' and 'gin' for 'begin'. • Consonant sounds that are similar to the ear are often confused, e.g. t/k/p, d/g/b, b/v.
2 years 6 months	• Vocabulary increases rapidly; there is less imbalance between passive and active vocabularies. • Word use is more specific so there are fewer over- and under-generalisations. • Sentences get longer and more precise, although they are still usually abbreviated versions of adult sentences. • Word order in sentences is sometimes incorrect but the meaning is evident. • Children can use language to protect their rights and interests and to maintain their own comfort and pleasure, e.g. 'It's mine', 'Get off'. • Children can listen to stories and are interested in them.

continued

3 years	• Vocabulary develops rapidly; words are picked up quickly. • Sentences continue to become longer and more like adult speech. • Children talk to themselves while playing to plan and order their play, which is evidence of children using language to think. • Stylistic variation (speaking differently in different contexts) is developing. • Language can now be used to report on what is happening, direct their own and others' actions, to express ideas and to initiate and maintain friendships. • Antonyms are often confused (early/late, today/yesterday) as children begin to engage with the meaning of more abstract words. • Pronouns are usually used correctly. • Questions are used frequently. • Rhymes and melody are attractive to children.
4 years	• Children's vocabulary is now extensive; new words are added regularly. • Longer and more complex sentences are used; sentences may be joined with 'because', which demonstrates a cognitive awareness of causes and relationships. • Children are able to narrate long stories, including the sequence of events. • Play involves running commentaries. • The boundaries between fact and fiction are blurred and this is reflected in speech. • Speech is fully intelligible with few, minor incorrect uses. • Questioning is at its peak. • Children can usually use language to: share, take turns, collaborate, argue, predict what may happen, compare possible alternatives, anticipate, give explanations, justify behaviour, create situations in imaginative play, reflect upon their own feelings and begin to describe how other people feel.
5 years	• Children have a wide range of vocabulary and can use it appropriately. • Vocabulary can include colours, shapes, numbers and common opposites. • Sentences are usually correctly structured, although incorrect grammar may still be used. • Pronunciation may still be childish. • Language continues to be used and developed, as described in the section on 4 year olds: this may now include phrases heard on the television and associated with children's toys. • Questions and discussions are for enquiry and information; questions become more precise as children's cognitive skills develop. • Children will offer opinions in discussion. • Children are still learning to understand ambiguities and subtleties in language, e.g. irony and metaphor.

Table 3.1: Developmental progression from birth to five years

From the age of five onwards children use, practise, adapt and refine their language knowledge and skill. They learn to use language for a wide variety of purposes as they move out from a world that is predominantly focused around the family and community into the world that is increasingly focused on school and peers. Joan Tough (1976) provides a useful way of understanding the uses of language that can be observed in children's spoken language as they use, adapt and refine their communicative skill. She describes seven uses of language. These uses are, she argues, hierarchical, beginning with the first stage of 'self-maintaining language' and progressing to 'imagining'. The earliest stages will be observable in most children's language by the age of five years.

Use	Using language to
1. Self-maintaining	**1.1** Protect oneself: • 'Stop it!' • 'Go away!' **1.2** Meet psychological and physical needs: • 'I'm thirsty.' • 'You're hurting me.'
2. Directing	**2.1** Direct actions of self and others: • 'You push the lorry round the track.' • 'I just need to put this brick here then I've finished.'
3. Reporting	**3.1** Label the component parts of a scene: • 'There is a car, a lorry and a bus.' **3.2** Refer to detail, colour, shape, size or position of an object **3.3** Talk about an incident **3.4** Refer to a sequence of events: • 'We walked to the bus stop and then caught the bus to school.' **3.5** Reflect on the meanings of experiences, including feelings: • 'I like playing in the shop, especially with Sarah.'
4. Towards logical reasoning	**4.1** Explain a process **4.2** Recognise causal and dependent relationships: • 'You have to put sugar in this tea or it's not very nice.' **4.3** Recognise problems and their causes. **4.4** Justify judgements and actions: • 'I didn't want to go out because I hadn't finished my drawing.'
5. Predicting	**5.1** Anticipate or forecast: • 'We're going to have a hamster and a cage with a wheel.' **5.2** Predict the consequences of actions or events: • 'That propeller will fall off if you don't stick it on properly.'
6. Projecting	**6.1** Project into the experiences, feelings and reactions of others: • 'He was stuck in there and couldn't get out and was frightened.' **6.2** Project into a situation never experienced: • 'I wouldn't like to be a rabbit and live in a cage, would you?'
7. Imagining	**7.1** Engage in play, in role, in an imagined context: • 'Hello, this is Hot Scissors hairdressers. Would you like to make an appointment?'

Table 3.2: Tough's seven uses of language

Critiques of a developmental approach

DEFINITION

Critique: critical analysis.

Critical analysis: an appraisal based on careful analytical evaluation.

One way of understanding theory is to see it as a filter through which our view of the world is formed. The theory acts as a filter allowing some things to be perceived and others not. This allows only some aspects of the world to impact on our understanding as we seek to interpret and understand that which we perceive.

Child development theory that underpins a developmental approach to children's growth and learning is one such filter in our perception of children and childhood. Dahlberg et al. (1999) describe this as 'the scientific child of biological stages'. The 'child' in child development theory is one whose development, regardless of context, follows a standard trajectory of often age-related stages. It is a child who is viewed as a series of identifiable and measurable areas of development: social, intellectual, physical and linguistic. It is a child who is viewed as one of a kind: a universal being waiting to be realised (James and Prout, 1997). Development in this conceptualisation of children is understood as an internal, individual process.

Age-related stages of development (which are informed by developmental psychological theory) are underpinned by the same assumptions. This is evident in the language development chart in Table 3.2. Language development is assumed to be linear, with staged progression linked to chronological age. It doesn't, in this form, take any account of a child's individual learning experiences. The chart lists norms, developmental parameters which can be used to make assessments of children's progress and check whether they match age-related descriptions. As aforementioned, this use of developmental ages and stages has clear practical use in the systems of health, education and social care as they are currently constructed.

ACTIVITY *1*

Assessing developmental progress

Joe, Mazara and Sophie are all at the end of the Foundation Stage. Their language development has been assessed against the stated criteria.

Joe 'uses talk to organise, sequence and clarify thinking, ideas, feelings and events'.

Mazara and Sophie are both able to 'initiate conversation with others, displaying greater confidence in more informal contexts.'

- *Based on these achievements, what is your assessment of these children's language development?*

- *State the reasons for your view.*

Joe is an only child of older parents. His mother has been at home with him. Before coming to school Joe and his mother have attended a range of groups: playgroups, singing groups and gym-tots. He arrived at school confident, able to talk with adults and children, and keen to be involved in all the activities on offer.

Mazara came to England with her parents six months ago. Her parents are both surgeons at the local hospital. They both speak fluent English but they have decided to speak Urdu at home with Mazara so that she maintains her home language. When she arrived in England, Mazara spoke no English.

continued

The use and the assumptions underpinning developmentalism are called into question in a number of ways.

The most persistent criticism of developmentalism is that it is decontextualised. That is, it doesn't allow for the different contexts in which children grow and learn. Developmentalism seeks to identify very broad, general patterns of development and apply these to *all* children regardless of their life experiences. Therefore, critics argue, it is too unsubtle an approach to understanding every child's growth and development. Additionally, the risk is that these normative descriptions of children's development provided by developmental psychology become prescriptions for what 'should' happen. The potential impact of this is two-fold: that they are used to classify and stratify individuals, groups and societies, and that they inform interventions to mould children into appropriate future citizens (Burman, 2008).

Burman (2008) argues that we need to think very carefully about these wider implications of a developmental approach, that we need to unpick, or deconstruct, the understandings that lie behind the approach. She is not challenging the detail of the theories that underpin developmental ages and stages but asking that we become aware of the ways in which these are used in society and the wider meanings and uses of developmentalism in society that are problematic.

Burman's critical analysis questions the assumption of developmental psychology as 'the truth'. She argues that there is a range of ideological assumptions within developmentalism that reflect a wider socio-political agenda.

- Whose development is being described and used as the measure for *all* children? Is it all children in all contexts? All classes, all cultures, girls and boys? If not, whose development has prominence and whose is not considered in the ages and stages outlined as developmental norms? Gilligan's work, outlined in Theory focus below, is a good example of this tension.

- Who is subject to intervention when developmental milestones are judged not to have been met?

Burman (2008) argues that it is the adequacy of mothering that developmental psychology is, in practice, used to judge. This is evidenced in the interventions that are designed to normalise children's development through services for children. In this way, a developmental approach is used to regulate families, mothers in particular, because a 'good mother' is defined in relation to her child in the context of the child's developmental progress. This seems particularly pertinent if the patterns of developmental progress used privilege some groups over others.

Burman reflects that, *we need to be vigilant about the range of intended and unintended effects mobilised by claims to development, mindful of whose development is being privileged and correspondingly, whose is marginalised* (2008:12).

THEORY FOCUS

Moral development

The following is an example of an unintended effect of developmental theory.

Kholberg, in developing his theory of moral development, presented 72 boys aged between 10 and 13 with a moral dilemma. He was interested in the reasoning behind their responses to the dilemma. From this reasoning he developed a stages theory of moral development which has been widely accepted. The stages are hierarchical.

Level 1: Pre-conventional morality

      Stage 1 – Obedience and punishment orientation

      Stage 2 – Individualism and exchange

Level 2: Conventional morality

      Stage 3 – Good interpersonal relationships

      Stage 4 – Maintaining the social order

Level 3: Post-conventional morality

      Stage 5 – Social contract and individual rights

      Stage 6 – Universal principles

Level 1 – At stage 1 children think of what is right as that which authority says is right. Doing the right thing is obeying authority and avoiding punishment. At stage 2, children see that there are different sides to any issue. Since everything is relative, one is free to pursue one's own interests, although it is often useful to make deals and exchange favours with others.

Level 2 – At stages 3 and 4, young people think as members of the conventional society with its values, norms and expectations. At stage 3, they emphasise being a good person, which means having helpful motives toward people to whom you are close. At stage 4, the concern shifts toward obeying laws to maintain society as a whole.

Level 3 – At stages 5 and 6 people are less concerned with maintaining society for its own sake, and more concerned with the principles and values that make for a good society. At stage 5 they emphasise basic rights and the democratic processes that give everyone a say, and at stage 6 they define the principles by which agreement will be just.

continued

THEORY FOCUS continued

This understanding of morality has been criticised by Gilligan (1982). Gilligan says that the stages are sex-biased. She observes that Kholberg's stages were developed exclusively from interviews with males and therefore embed a male view of morality that centres around rules, rights and abstract principles.

Gilligan's work demonstrates that women's morality centres much more around interpersonal relationships and the ethics of care, compassion and maintaining relationships. It is about real, lived, ongoing relationships and the associated ways of living that achieve this rather than abstract ideas. Therefore, in Kholberg's stages of moral development women typically score at stage 3, while the highest stages are reserved for more male ways of thinking.

Conclusion

For the practitioner whose role often requires that they make normative developmental assessments, the way in which developmental charts are used is crucial in addressing some of the outlined concerns. If the principles outlined at the start of this chapter are applied each time developmental assessments are undertaken, if they are used reflectively with an awareness that there is a range of issues around their underpinning assumptions, and if they are used reflexively, with an awareness of practitioners' own understandings and views, then developmental assessment can be a more nuanced, personalised, relevant and therefore useful process.

SUMMARY

This chapter has outlined the developmental stages of language development and has identified a range of principles that underpin the use of developmental assessment in early years. Criticisms of developmentalism have been identified, including questions about underpinning assumptions, how these have influenced the development of theory and how they may impact on assessments made. A principled, reflective and reflexive approach to using developmental stages is identified as a means by which practitioners can assess children's development in a way that is relevant and useful to the individual child.

FURTHER READING

Blenkly, MF, Tarule, J, Goldberger, N and Clinchy, B (1986) *Women's Ways of Knowing: The Development of Self, Voice and Mind*. New York: Basic Books.

Burman, E (2008) *Deconstructing Developmental Psychology*. London: Routledge.

Edwards, C, Gandidi, L and Forman, G (1998) *The Hundred Languages of Children*. New Jersey: Ablex Publishing Corporation.

Gilligan, C (1982) *In a Different Voice. Psychological Theory and Women's Development*. London: Harvard University Press.

James, A and Prout, A (1997) *Constructing and Reconstructing Childhood. Contemporary Issues in the Sociological Study of Childhood*. London: RoutledgeFalmer.

Layard, R and Dunn, J (2009) *A Good Childhood. Searching for Values in a Competitive Age*. London: Penguin.

Moss, P and Petrie, P (2002) *From Children's Services to Children's Spaces: Public Policy, Children and Childhood*. London. RoutledgeFalmer.

Prout, A (2005) *The Future of Childhood*. London: RoutledgeFalmer.

Pugh, G and Duffy, B (2006) *Contemporary Issues in the Early Years*. London: SAGE.

Saxton, M (2010) *Child Language. Acquisition and Development*. London: SAGE.

4   Talking with babies

This chapter enables you to understand:

- why talking to babies is important;
- positive strategies for talking with babies.

Introduction

Consider how people interact with babies. What do you notice about this interaction? Why do you think we interact in this way? What assumptions about babies' capabilities in communication and language underpin this interaction? How do babies respond to this interaction? What does this tell you about babies' communicative abilities?

Language acquisition begins in the earliest days of life as people communicate with the baby through smiling, gazing, singing and chatting. Instinctively, we enter into this social relationship with the assumption that the baby is interested in, and capable of, communication with us. Indeed, we often engage with babies as if they are participating in the interaction by anticipating and modelling their contribution in the interaction. Babies respond reciprocally to these communicative acts in various ways; through becoming still and listening, through eye contact and gazing and, as they grow and develop, through whole body movements and vocalisations. This is evidence of a strong internal drive for babies to engage in communication and enter into social interaction. These powerful social communicative interactions are the beginnings of language acquisition and, if nurtured, will enable a child to acquire and develop spoken language with ease.

ACTIVITY 1

Watching babies communicate

Log onto Youtube and search for clips of talking with babies. There are some fabulous examples of babies' powerful drive to communicate.

Notice:

- *their eye contact;*
- *their facial expression;*
- *how attentive and engaged they are;*
- *how they respond with their whole body;*

continued

- *how they enter into social interaction through smiles and vocalisations;*

- *the adult's tone of voice;*

- *the shortened sentences and repetitive use of words;*

- *how the adult 'fills in' the baby's part of the communication;*

- *the delight of both baby and parent in the interaction.*

Why talking with babies is important

Talking with babies enables them to develop communication and language skills. Language and communication are learned skills. They are learned through social interaction with others (see Chapters 2, 3 and 5). This ability to acquire and use language is vital to our participation in society and these earliest years in a child's life are an important and sensitive time in learning and developing these skills. Communicating with babies and young children is important for a number of reasons.

- There is a link between the quantity and quality of the language that a child hears and their language acquisition and development.

- Early interaction affects brain development.

- Early interaction is an important part of bonding and attachment.

- Early communication through gesture (non-verbal communication) is significant in the acquisition and development of spoken language.

The impact of the quality and quantity of interaction on language development

Research shows that there is a powerful link between the *quantity* and the *quality* of language and interaction that babies and very young children experience in the home and their acquisition and development of communication and language skills (Sylva et al., 2004; Snow, 2001; Locke et al., 2002; Hart and Risley, 1995).

One such study by Hart and Risley (1995) highlights the importance of talking with babies and young children. Hart and Risley sought to understand why some children were slower to develop their language than others and why their development remained behind other groups of children. They concluded that the children's language, in both groups, reflected the *quantity* of language that they were exposed to in their earliest years; the children with good language development had been exposed to high levels of language and interaction while the children with poorer language development had been exposed to lower levels of language and interaction. Hart and Risley (1995) estimated that by the time the children were three years old the language gap between the two groups was 30 million words.

Kathy Sylva and colleagues (2003) demonstrated that the *quality* of interaction between parents and children supported their development. They found that what parents do is more important than who they are in supporting children's development. The study (EPPE, 2003) found that development was enhanced by parents talking, singing, reading and playing with their children, and it is this *quality* interaction, particularly at home, that was related to later positive outcomes in school.

This research demonstrates the importance of both the quantity and quality of interaction with babies; that we need to tune into their drive and capacity to communicate with us and include talking and singing as frequent and vital aspects of their daily experiences.

CASE STUDY

Supporting the development of communication in daily routines

A group was set up in a children's centre to support parents with weaning their babies. The staff agreed that this would be an excellent opportunity to introduce ideas for talking with your baby during this daily routine. The staff decided to use humour to communicate their message. They acted out a range of 'feeding scenarios' to get parents to think about and discuss which approach is most likely to support a child's language and communication skills.

- *Mum feeds the baby while having a conversation with a friend. There is no attention given to the baby or eye contact made while feeding.*

- *Mum puts on a video to amuse the child while feeding; there is no communication between mum and baby.*

- *Baby has a range of toys on a highchair tray. The baby is distracted by the toys and not interested in the food or her mum's chat.*

- *Mum feeds silently.*

- *Mum keeps up a stream of excited chatter leaving no time for the baby to respond.*

- *Mum is in a hurry, feeds too fast, doesn't pick up cues as to when baby is ready for next mouthful – baby gags and chokes.*

- *Mum is sensitive and responsive to baby's feeding cues, minimises distractions and has a 'conversation' with the baby including turn-taking and 'filling in' the baby's contribution.*

The parents enjoyed that the message was delivered with humour and were able to identify why the final scenario is most likely to support their child's development. Each parent then chose one of the ideas that they had seen to do when feeding the baby in the following week. Staff felt that they had communicated their message clearly and modelled effective ways to talk with a baby during daily routines.

Adapted from Blaydon Winlaton 'Baby Bites' at www.literacytrust.org.uk

Early interaction and brain development

There is increasing evidence of the importance of early stimulation on the development of the brain (National Scientific Council on the Developing Child, 2005, 2008, 2011). The brain develops through the interplay of nature and nurture. This means that all babies are born with significant potential and a drive to learn and develop but it is their experiences after they are born that determine their actual learning. Babies and young children who receive warm, responsive, developmentally appropriate care are likely to flourish. This developmentally appropriate care includes interaction with parents, siblings and other family and community members; talk, singing, reading and play.

Studies of how these early interactions stimulate connections in the brain (neuroscience) show that early stimulation is highly significant in children's development. The brain consists of billions of neurons. It is the complex networks of connections between these neurons that result in learning. At birth the brain has established initial connections and pathways between these neurons. The flood of sensory experiences that a child receives begins the process of creating complex neural pathways and connections. Importantly, studies of the brain show that early stimulation is particularly significant in developing these connections. These early years are often referred to as 'sensitive' or 'critical' periods in a child's development, when the brain is at its most flexible and responsive to stimulation. Talking, singing, playing and reading with babies is an important part of the flood of sensory experiences necessary as stimulation for the child in this early critical phase of brain development.

Language development is a good example of the way in which our brains shape and reshape themselves depending upon our experiences. Almost all children learn to speak but which language(s) they speak will depend entirely upon their exposure to a particular language and their brain will shape itself to the language(s) heard. For example, it will create connections that enable recognition of the sounds that occur in the language(s) that is heard and, conversely, not create connections for sounds that don't appear in the language(s) heard. More importantly, it seems logical that the more language that a child is exposed to, the greater the number of neural connections so the greater the child's language capability. This understanding of brain development would support Hart and Risley's research findings outlined above.

THEORY FOCUS

What is meant by a sensitive or critical time to learn?

A critical or sensitive period for learning refers to a genetically determined period of growth during which the system is especially plastic, in the sense that it is especially receptive to particular environmental inputs. Critical periods act as a window of opportunity for development. If development doesn't occur during this period, it may not be possible thereafter (Saxton, 2010).

continued

There is still some debate about the nature of sensitive periods in language learning. Studies have focused on profound linguistic deprivation, for example, feral children, on second language acquisition and on late language learning, for example, children who are born deaf. None are conclusive, but on balance the evidence suggests that there is a critical period in early childhood when, unless children acquire their first language effectively, it becomes much more difficult to achieve this later.

Talking with babies, bonding and attachment

Talking and singing with babies, along with early eye contact, gazing, holding and touching, particularly skin-to-skin touch, are ways in which parents and children can establish warm, responsive and loving relationships; this is part of creating a bond of attachment. Attachment is an emotional bond to another person. It emerges from the special relationship that involves an exchange of comfort, care and pleasure between a young child and their parents and/or other significant carer. The central tenet of attachment theory (Bowlby, 1953) is that mothers who are available and responsive to their babies' needs establish a sense of security. The baby learns that the mother is dependable, which creates a secure base for the child to move out into the world and engage their exploratory impulses with confidence. There is also evidence to suggest that the process of bonding begins prior to birth as babies can hear and respond to familiar voices. So, communication with a child, both verbal and non-verbal, prior to birth and after, can contribute to a strong bond of attachment between parents and children.

The importance of gesture in communication

There is increasing evidence about the role of gesture in children's language acquisition and development. Gesture refers to a child's non-verbal communication, pointing, waving, clapping and whole body movements. A number of research studies have found that there is a relationship between babies and young children's use of gesture and the development of language. Communicative gesture has been shown to be a good predictor of vocabulary size and of the development of receptive and expressive language (Desrochers et al., 1995; Rowe et al., 2005: Iverson and Golin-Meadow, 2005).

Additionally, Tomasello (2003) in his usage-based theory of language acquisition would argue that the process of intention reading in gesture enables young children to acquire the appropriate use of communicative symbols which eventually lead to the use of more complex linguistic expressions and constructions (see Chapter 2).

Positive strategies for talking with babies

Interaction requires that at least two people are engaged with one another. As babies have limited capabilities to initiate this interaction it requires that other people engage with the baby to support and develop the baby's communicative skills.

The National Literacy Trust's Face to Face research (2010) identified three key areas that contribute to effective communication with babies:

- contingency: babies and parents or carers being 'tuned in' to reciprocal communication;

- the nature and types of parent-baby interaction;

- the importance of the home literacy environment.

Contingency

Contingency refers to the level of reciprocal communication produced in an interaction between baby and parent. It means that the parent and baby are fully orientated towards the interaction, that they are both cueing into and responding to one another.

These high levels of joint attention and reciprocity are associated with more effective communication and, in turn, with more rapid child language development. This synthesis of research evidence concluded that parents who take their lead from their children in this way are more effective than those who directed them, and that mothers who frequently respond verbally to their children's play and vocalisations supplied their children with more effective and nuanced language models than those who responded occasionally.

Parent-baby interaction

Some of the ways in which parents and babies interact have been shown to be effective in supporting children's communication and language skills, such as:

- gesture;

- meaningful interaction;

- use of an elaborated way of talking;

- the home literacy environment.

Gesture is important. It precedes language and is indicative of a baby's language and cognitive skill, for example, communicative pointing or waving bye-bye to a prompt. These early gestures have been linked with good receptive and expressive language development (National Literacy Trust, 2010). This requires that parents (and practitioners) are aware of children's use of gesture as a communicative act and that they respond accordingly. The response is required to enable the communication to be a successful two-way process, which in turn will encourage children to continue to use gesture to communicate as they acquire and develop their spoken language.

Talk with babies that enhances communication and language skill is talk that has a meaningful context: daily events, interesting things that happen and recalling things that have happened. At its most effective, interaction with babies and very young children should explain and elaborate on routines and events, ask questions and seek to construct an understanding with the child. This more detailed interaction, rather than simply description, leads to more contextual information for the child, more use of questioning and a wider use of vocabulary. This means that the child is exposed to more language, both more vocabulary and more complex language constructions, which in turn has an impact on children's language acquisition (NLT, 2010; Hart and Risley, 1995).

An elaborated style of talking that combines a particular communicative style with detailed content (as outlined above) has been shown to have an impact on children's language acquisition. An effective style of interaction is one in which the way that you speak is exaggerated: intonation, pitch, pace and facial expression are all made more dynamic in the interaction. This elaborated communicative style is sometimes referred to as Motherese or child-directed speech (CDS). It is the way in which mothers (and other adults) can be observed talking with a child.

THEORY FOCUS

Motherese/child-directed speech

Motherese refers to the simplified and repetitive type of speech, with exaggerated intonation and rhythm, often used by adults when speaking to babies. It is also referred to as child-directed speech (CDS). CDS is the speech that you hear adults use with babies and young children. It is clearly recognisable as this: an adult talking to a child. CDS is regarded as *facilitative* of language acquisition and development rather than necessary to language acquisition and development.

CDS includes:

- exaggerated intonation, swooping curves of sound over an extended pitch range;

- a higher overall pitch;

- slower speech;

- a lengthening of syllables;

- longer pauses;

- the choice of more concrete, easily understood words;

- *object* words put at the end of a sentence and emphasised through saying them more loudly;

- sentences that tend to be shortened but remain grammatically correct.

(Saxton, 2010)

There is no clear understanding as to why adults use this way of talking with babies and young children. It has been suggested that it is more dynamic and therefore children are attracted and responsive to this mode of speaking. Interestingly, there are studies that show that CDS is used in a range of different social and cultural contexts, particularly within a child's first year of life. This suggests that these adaptations in the way we speak to very young children are perhaps more than a social or culturally defined practice.

The home literacy environment refers to the range of literacy practices in the home which children see modelled and with which they join in. This includes using talk, reading and writing for pleasure and work and as practices embedded in everyday life and routines. Evidence shows that children's language acquisition and development is enhanced by greater exposure to, and involvement in, these practices in their everyday life and routines, for example:

- high levels of talk about events and in daily routines;

- story-telling;

- encouraging active listening by drawing children's attention to sounds and rhymes;

- symbolic play such as role play and small world;

- shared book reading;

- singing and reciting rhymes;

- visits to the library or museums.

Although the Face to Face study (NLT, 2010) was focused on parents, the same processes are effective for babies in daycare; staff need to engage in meaningful, individual, focused and reciprocal communication. In daycare this requires that the room and staffing are organised to enable this to be an important part of each day. Staff need to be aware of the importance of communication with babies and young children and plan time for talking. There is a risk that in a busy daycare setting time to talk gets squeezed in alongside everything else and so takes place in unfocused short bursts as staff divide their time and attention between their many tasks. Similarly, staff need to provide a literate environment for the children in their care. As well as time to talk this includes: providing play activities that enable and encourage talk and communication; engaging in singing and teaching children nursery rhymes; encouraging babies and young children to listen carefully by drawing their attention to sounds and modelling focused listening; and reading books and telling stories. All of this is crucial if children's language and communication skills are to thrive. Babies and young children need to grow and develop within a literate environment in which focused, engaged talk, which is sensitive to their changing developmental needs, is an important part of each day.

CASE STUDY

Time to talk in a daycare setting

Staff in a baby room were aware of the importance of talking with babies to support their language acquisition. However, through their discussions and observations they began to realise that they spent very little time in focused talk with the babies. They noticed that the talk seemed to be in short bursts, often a quick comment on what was happening as they passed by. Similarly, changing and feeding times had become increasingly rushed and so time to talk during these daily routines was limited.

continued

CASE STUDY *continued*

The staff decided that they needed to alter the staff and room organisation so that time to talk was made a priority each day. Firstly, staff reviewed the learning environment to ensure that there were opportunities for practitioners and the babies and young children to engage in listening and talking. They made a number of changes to their provision. For example, they:

- *included more photographs of the children in books and displays around the room;*
- *created basket of resources that practitioners could use to encourage listening, including books, puppets, taped stories and a treasure basket of things that made sounds;*
- *created a basket of percussion instruments to take outside in the garden;*
- *put wind chimes in the tree above a bench in the garden;*
- *set aside an area in the garden to grow some flowers and vegetables;*
- *put pictures up in the garden of common birds and insects;*
- *put some mirrors and wind chimes in the changing area.*

Next, staff reviewed their work patterns and adapted them to ensure that each day each key worker had time to spend in focused talking time with each individual child in their group. They agreed that:

- *each day each member of staff would have time when their task was to engage in a focused talking and/or listening time with each of the children in their group. This time was to be spent focused on talking with the child while engaged in the activities on offer;*
- *in the time spent with each child staff should focus on the individual child, ensuring that their interaction remained sensitive to the child's changing ability through careful observation;*
- *lunch time would be extended and more staff would be involved so that more time could be spent talking with each child as they ate.*

Finally, they agreed to work in this way for three months and then review how it was working. Did it offer them more time to talk with the children? Was the talk more focused? Did they think that children were benefiting from this provision? What else could they do to make the time-to-talk work better for the children?

SUMMARY

This chapter has outlined the importance of talking with babies and young children. It has identified that this is important because language is a skill that is learned in social relationships and that early childhood is a 'sensitive' or 'critical' time to learn to talk. A number of reasons why talking to babies is important have been identified and discussed: that the quality and quantity of language that a child hears is linked to their language

continued

SUMMARY *continued*

*ability; that early interaction is crucial to brain development; that interaction is an impor-
tant part of the bonding and attachment process and that the earliest communicative acts
through gesture are significant in language development. Positive strategies for interacting with babies and young children in the home are discussed and then linked to working
with babies in a daycare setting.*

FURTHER READING

Brock, A and Rankin, C (2008) *Communication, Language and Literacy from Birth to Five*. London: SAGE.

Goodwin, P (2008) *Understanding Children's Books*. London: SAGE.

Hart, B and Risley, TR (1995) *Meaningful Differences in the Everyday Experience of Young American Children* (revised January 2003). Baltimore, MD, USA: Brookes Publishing.

Roulstone, S, Law, J, Rush, R, Clegg, J and Peters, T (2010) Investigating the role of language in children's early educational outcomes. Available at www.education.gov.uk/publications/ eOrderingDownload/DFE-RR134.pdf, accessed 30.04.12

Saxton, M (2010) *Child Language. Acquisition and Development*. London: SAGE.

Whitehead, M (2002) *Developing Language and Literacy with Young Children*. London: Paul Chapman Press.

WEBSITES

www.ican.org.uk

www.literacytrust.org.uk/talk_to_your_baby

5   Factors that affect children's language acquisition and development

This chapter enables you to understand:

• how levels of interaction affect language acquisition and development;
• how language acquisition may be affected in children who have special educational needs;
• TV and language acquisition and development.

Introduction

Earlier chapters in this book have outlined how learning language is a combination of genetic sensitivity to language and exposure to, and involvement in, spoken language. Language acquisition occurs through the interplay of genetic potential and social interaction. Put simply:

> ### Every **LAD** needs a **LASS**
>
> or
>
> Every **L**anguage **A**cquisition **D**evice needs a **L**anguage **A**cquisition **S**upport **S**ystem.

It naturally follows therefore that if either the potential to acquire and develop language and/or the quality of social interaction are compromised in any way then language acquisition will be affected. We can also assume that the impact of the different factors that affect language acquisition will vary according to the type and severity of the issue.

It is impossible to unpick the exact impact of any one factor on language acquisition and development as each child is individual and will be affected differently. However, it is observable that, as children grow and learn, some factors can be identified as having an impact on language acquisition and development.

The level and quality of interaction

There is a powerful relationship between the quality and quantity of language exposure and language learned. There is evidence from practitioners, from research, and from national attainment statistics that there is a significant relationship between language acquisition and ability, and learning. Language impacts on all aspects of our life and learning; it determines our ability to understand, our ability to communicate our ideas and learning (through spoken language and literacy), to understand and communicate our needs, and to form and maintain personal, social and professional relationships. Therefore, the greater our ability with language the better equipped we are to engage in learning across all aspects of our lives. This process starts with the acquisition of spoken language in the early years of life.

Hart and Risley's (1995) research showed exactly this: how early language experiences impact on language acquisition and development and how this in turn has an impact on later outcomes for children, particularly in terms of their educational attainment. Hart and Risley identified a significant gap in the volume of language heard by children growing up in different homes. They estimated the gap between children's exposure to language in homes where there was a lot of talk and homes where there was less talk was up to 32 million words in the first three years of life. Their research also revealed that, as well as the quantity of the language heard, children who had high exposure to language also heard more complex language. They found that all parents used a similar number of imperatives (*come here*) and prohibitions (*stop doing that*) and questions (*what are you doing?*). However, the data showed that when parents engaged in more talk than was necessary to communicate these imperatives, prohibitions and questions the quality of the talk changed. Parents moved into discussing feelings, plans, present activities and past events, and the vocabulary became more varied and the descriptions richer and more nuanced. The consequence of the fact that *more language* was used in the home was that the language that children were exposed to and engaged in was *significantly richer* because parents elaborated on what they wanted to communicate.

It is important to be aware that simple exposure to spoken language, without participation, isn't sufficient for effective language acquisition and development. Children need to be actively involved in using language and gesture to communicate; language is acquired through social *interaction.* This social interaction is the child's language acquisition support system (LASS).

Other research confirms the conclusions of Hart and Risley. The National Literacy Trust's Face to Face project observed that 'talkative parents have talkative children'. Their research concluded that there is robust and substantial evidence across cultures of the effect of socio-economic status (SES) on language learning environments; this includes the amount of talk in the home. SES is a term used to describe a range of social factors in people's lives, such as where you live, level of qualification, income and occupation. Research shows that, generally speaking, mothers in homes of a higher SES talk more to their children than mothers from homes that have a lower SES. In the homes with a higher SES mothers talked more frequently to begin and maintain conversation, opening up communication and elaborating on what was happening and why, whereas mothers in homes with a lower SES talked more to direct their children's behaviour resulting in communication that is less elaborated. Similarly, the age and mental health of mothers has shown to be significant in communication: very young mothers have been shown to communicate less frequently with their children and engage in directive communication to organise and manage behaviour. Depressed mothers, similarly, engage in less communication that is 'tuned in' to their child.

> ### DEFINITION
>
> Socio-economic status (SES): The term 'socio-economic status' is generally used to identify a person's status relative to others based on characteristics such as income, qualifications, type of occupation and where they live. As a result, a number of measures have been developed to classify people into groups based on different characteristics. These measures are used to assess inequalities between social groups. Socio-economic status is usually understood as a multi-dimensional concept.
>
> Socio-economic group: A way of classifying people that groups them with others of similar social and economic status. The classifications are used by the Office for National Statistics.
>
> Indices of deprivation: The Index of Multiple Deprivation combines a number of indicators, chosen to cover a range of economic, social and housing issues, into a single deprivation score for each small area in England. This allows each area to be ranked relative to others according to their level of deprivation. It is used as one of the indicators of SES.

What this research demonstrates is that there are very positive outcomes in terms of language acquisition and development for children who grow up in talkative homes; homes where there is high lexical frequency and (perhaps therefore) high lexical diversity accompanied by frequent, relevant gesture that supports communication.

Saxton (2010) adds some detail as to why children from talkative households tend to have talkative children. Talkative parents use longer, syntactically more complex utterances. This benefits the child's acquisition of complex grammar (Vasilyeva et al., 2008) so these children use more complex grammar earlier and this has been shown to persist over time (Hoff, 2006). Children with talkative parents have also been shown to have wider vocabularies and consequently be more effective at processing speech (Hurtado et al., 2008). This in turn enables them to acquire language quickly and efficiently and so sets up a positive pattern: the early ability to use language has a positive impact on language acquisition and development which, in turn, has a positive impact on the ability to use language, which has a positive effect on language acquisition and development.

Important issues to consider

While a family's socio-economic status has been shown to have an impact on a child's language acquisition it is important to remember that these are general conclusions. There is inevitably variation between families whatever their SES and while these general conclusions may be useful for policy makers it is important that as practitioners we base our judgements on what we observe of children in our care rather than make pre-judgements based on what we know of the external factors in a child's life. This approach is in accordance with one of the important findings of the EPPE study (Sylva et al., 2003). The study found that it is the quality of the home learning environment that promotes development rather than parental occupation or qualification: it is more important what a parent does than who they are.

The Effective Provision of Pre-School Education (EPPE) Study

In addition to existing evidence on the impact of early learning on children's development the Labour government (1999–2007) commissioned research to investigate the effects of pre-school education and explore the characteristics of effective practice. It is called the EPPE study (the Effective Provision of Pre-School Education). The study ran from 1997 to 2003. It found that attending pre-school had many beneficial effects on children's development, particularly for children who came from disadvantaged backgrounds. The study also found that integrated settings – those that provided education and care – were most effective in supporting development and achieving good outcomes for children. A follow-up study published in 2009 found that the quality of pre-school provision can moderate the impact of risks to a child's cognitive development. The outcomes from the study have been very influential in shaping governmental early years policy.

It is also important to consider issues behind the current concern about children's language acquisition and development. When we talk about children having poor language development, what do we mean? Poor, by which measure? By 'poor' do we mean that a child's language acquisition and development is affecting their ability to communicate within their family and community, or is it about their ability to manage the demands of early schooling? Is it pre-dominantly about the child or the system? If many children do seem unable to manage the demands of the early years of schooling what should change? Currently, we seem to assume that it is a within-child problem and seek to solve the disparity by trying to accelerate children's development. Could we argue that the early years of schooling should be more attuned to the inevitable differences in children's development?

It is also worth considering that the demands made of very young children in the early years of school in the UK are very different to those made of children in a number of European countries where they don't start formal schooling until the age of six or seven. In the system as it is currently conceived, children in the UK are expected to be sufficiently adept at speaking and listening to move into reading and writing by the age of six or seven. Who do you think is right? Which developmental patterns and expectations are appropriate? By what measures are we making judgements in this country about children's language (and literacy) development and are these appropriate? Whose needs are foregrounded in our current system?

Expectations: how do they affect what we expect?

Georgia is four years old. She had recently moved to live in Munich with her family and attended a German kindergarten (nursery for children aged 4–6) each morning. At Christmas she made some cards for her new friends at the kindergarten. She drew pictures on the front and decorated them with glitter. Inside she attempted to write 'Happy Christmas, love from Georgia'. This took some time and a lot of effort as Georgia had only just begun to learn to hold a pencil correctly and form letters in her Reception class before she left England to live in Munich. She had to copy the words and some of the letters consisted of sticks and balls in a rough approximation of the letter.

She handed out the cards to her German friends at kindergarten, some of whom showed the cards to their parents at home time. The German parents were slightly bewildered and asked Georgia's mum about the writing inside. They were amazed and concerned that in England children as young as Georgia were required to write. Their view was that this was developmentally inappropriate. Children of this age were much too young to be writing. They said that kindergarten was a time for learning to talk, interact and play and that formalising knowledge and skill in this way was not appropriate for young children. Writing was something that they would learn in school when they started at age six, seven or even eight years old as the exact age that a child would start school would depend on an assessment of their maturity.

- *What do you think about the German mothers' response?*

- *What do we mean by developmentally appropriate?*

- *What social and cultural factors affect our expectations?*

- *What are the implications of this for the labels that we give to children who don't meet (or exceed) our expectations?*

- *What is the potential impact of the labels that we give children?*

Children who have special educational needs

Communication and language acquisition and development is often affected in children who have special educational needs. The extent to which a child is affected will depend upon their individual needs and abilities. A child's needs, including language needs, may be anything from short term, and ameliorated through intervention and support, to lifelong and pervasive.

As language is such a vital aspect of our ability to communicate and learn, when children's language acquisition and development are affected it follows that learning and communication will be similarly affected. The extent to which these aspects of a child's development are affected will vary according to the individual child's needs and abilities.

The impact of special educational needs on language acquisition and development

Sam has a diagnosis of autism. He has no spoken language. Sam often knows exactly what he wants and becomes frustrated if he cannot make himself understood. This includes throwing equipment and himself around the room.

Sam understands simple language (key words) in the context of his familiar daily routine, for example sit down, coat, snack time, drink. Sam's parents and staff at his school use Makaton signs and symbols alongside these key words to aid communication.

Sam has also recently been introduced to an AAC device (Augmentative Alternative Communication device): a GO Talk 20. This is a grid with 20 squares that contain a mixture of photographs, symbols and pictures. The device is programmed with the spoken word so when Sam chooses and presses a square he hears a spoken word. Sam has different grids for different times in the day and for different activities. This device enables Sam to make choices and indicate his needs, for example, which snack he'd prefer or that he needs a drink. As the AAC device has enabled better communication between Sam and others it has alleviated some of his frustrations at not being able to communicate his needs, make choices and express preferences.

Television and language development

The relationship between television watching and young children's language development is an interesting one. The television is a feature of almost all children's lives and most children will watch television during the early years of their lives when they are learning to talk. The 'common-sense' view may be one that children hear a lot of talking when watching television so it is beneficial to their language acquisition and development. However, the effect of television watching on very young children's language acquisition and development is less clear and more complex than this. Research shows that the benefits of television watching relative to language acquisition are age related and linked to a *particular type of viewing* of a *particular type of programme*. The evidence across research (Close, 2004) suggests that:

- children between the ages of two and five years old may benefit from watching high-quality educational programmes that are age-appropriate;

- there is almost no evidence of benefit for language acquisition from television watching for children under two years of age;

- viewing by children of programmes aimed at a general or adult audience is correlated with poor language development in pre-school aged children;

- children who are heavy viewers of television are more likely to be linguistically underdeveloped (although a direct causal relationship has not been established so other factors may also be involved).

THEORY FOCUS

Further findings on television and children's language development

Programmes that support young children's language development have a number of characteristics. They:

- are age appropriate;

- include both new and familiar words;

- offer possibilities for interaction;

- offer minimal visual and auditory stimulation;

- maintain a balance between new and familiar words and use some sophisticated language;

- contain material that encourages interest and participation through songs, rhymes and questions.

In terms of the quantity of television watched and its relationship to early language development, children who are heavy viewers of television are more likely to be linguistically underdeveloped. Higher rates of television watching are correlated with:

- the availability of televisions in the home;

- particular family circumstances, such as low education of parents, young parents, low SES of the family and male gender of the child.

Where televisions are located in children's bedrooms, this is associated with reduced opportunities for co-viewing with parents, and greater exposure to the viewing of adult/general programmes.

Source: Close (2004).

SUMMARY

This chapter has discussed the factors that affect language acquisition and development. It has been argued that if we understand language acquisition and development as a combination of a genetic sensitivity to language and exposure to, and participation in, spoken language then where these aspects of a child's growth and development are affected their language development will be similarly affected. Two factors that are known to affect children's language acquisition and development have been identified

continued

SUMMARY *continued*

and discussed: the level and quality of interaction and having special educational needs. The impact of television viewing on language acquisition and development has also been highlighted and research evidence cited that shows that only certain types of viewing of certain types of programmes can be shown to be beneficial to children's language acquisition. Questions have been raised in the chapter about our current expectations of children's language acquisition and comparisons made with children in different countries where there are different expectations regarding spoken language and the move into literacy. It has been highlighted that it is not possible to unpick the exact impact of any one factor on language acquisition and development as each child is individual and will be affected differently.

FURTHER READING

Saxton, M (2010) *Child Language. Acquisition and Development*. London: SAGE.

Roulstone, S, Law, J, Rush, R, Clegg, J and Peters, T (2010) *Investigating the Role of Language in Children's Early Educational Outcomes*. Available at www.education.gov.uk/publications/eOrderingDownload/DFE-RB134.pdf, accessed 29.02.12.

Whitehead, M (2010) *Language and Literacy in the Early Years 0–7*. 4th Edition. London: SAGE.

WEBSITES

www.literacytrust.org.uk

6 Responding to children with speech, language and communication needs

This chapter enables you to understand:

- what we mean by speech, language and communication needs;
- how practitioners and teachers can respond to children with these needs.

What are speech, language and communication needs?

'Speech, language and communication needs' refers to a range of difficulties associated with the acquisition and development of language for communication and thinking. In this context speech, language and communication have specific meanings.

- *Speech* refers to the sounds that we produce that make up our language (or languages). Some children experience difficulties with the pronunciation of sounds which makes their speech (expressive language) difficult to understand.

- *Language* refers to the structure of the language (or languages) spoken; grammar, vocabulary, semantics and pragmatics. Some children have difficulties with understanding and/or structuring their speech in a way that enables them to communicate effectively.

- *Communication* refers to the ability to communicate with others through a range of verbal, non-verbal, signed or recorded means. Some children have difficulties in understanding and engaging in effective communication with others.

Children can experience a range of difficulties which may include one, some or all of the aspects of language listed above. There is perhaps a distinction to be made between children who have delayed language development but who don't experience any specific difficulties and children for whom a specific aspect of their language development is affected. However, all children, whether they have language delay or specific speech, language and communication difficulties will benefit from intervention by skilled, knowledgeable practitioners who are able to help them and their families support their language learning.

> ### DEFINITION
>
> Expressive language: the use of words and sentences to communicate with others.
>
> Receptive language: the ability to understand words and sentences that are used by others to communicate.
>
> Grammar: the system and structure of a language which determines how words are combined into clauses and sentences.
>
> Vocabulary: the words that we know and use.
>
> Semantics: an understanding of the meanings of words, phrases, sentences or texts.
>
> Pragmatics: the recognition and appropriate use of language in different forms (for example, a question) and in different ways according to the situation.

Why do some children have speech, language and communication difficulties?

Factors that can be identified as affecting language acquisition and development include the quantity and quality of interaction as a child learns language, and the impact of a child's special educational needs (these have been discussed in detail in Chapter 5). This accords with government guidance (DCSF, 2008) which highlights six possible causes of speech, language and communication difficulties:

- ear infections – when children have repeated ear infections it may affect their ability to hear;

- specific difficulties in using oral muscles effectively which may affect speech – for example, if a child has cerebral palsy;

- problems during pregnancy or at birth that affect children's developing brains and contribute to speech, language and communication difficulties as part of a wider developmental delay;

- difficulties that are passed down through families;

- a recognised syndrome or disorder that causes communication difficulties, such as autism;

- a lack of stimulation and support to provide the language experiences necessary to develop speech, language and communication skills.

For most children there is no clear, identifiable cause. However, knowing and articulating the cause of a child's difficulties is only a part of the picture. What is observable is that children who experience difficulties with their speech, their language and/or their communication are likely to face barriers to engaging in social interaction that builds relationships and enables learning. Knowing why the child is experiencing these difficulties tells us what may have happened in the past. What seems to be more important in supporting children's language learning is working out what needs to happen in the future (although in some cases knowing why a child is experiencing difficulties may inform the way forward).

So, in this context, what seems particularly useful is the clear identification of a child's needs, through observation and assessment, so that the right intervention and support can be offered.

Working with children who have speech, language and communication needs

Children acquire and develop their language from interaction with the people around them. This means that when children are experiencing difficulties with their language and communication it is the people around them, their family and community, including staff at their pre-school and school, who are best placed to notice and support children's needs. When children have speech, language and communication difficulties it is vital that practitioners are able to identify this as early as possible and respond to the child's needs.

Practitioners working with young children need the knowledge and skill to be able to:

- recognise children's needs;

- respond appropriately and effectively.

Recognising children's speech, language and communication needs

Practitioners need a range of professional knowledge and skill to enable them to recognise when children's acquisition and development of language is outside expectations and is having an impact on the child's overall development. Practitioners need to:

- know how children acquire and develop language;

- be aware of factors that affect children's language acquisition and development;

- know the expected language developmental parameters;

- know what is meant by speech, language and communication difficulties;

- have an understanding of holistic development and therefore the impact of speech, language and communication difficulties on other aspects of children's learning.

This range of knowledge and skills will enable practitioners to identify children who have language needs. There is evidence to suggest (Allen and Duncan Smith, 2008) that early intervention with children who have additional needs offers the best chance of effective intervention. Therefore the sooner practitioners can identify needs and begin the process of focused support the more likely that the intervention will be successful.

Responding to children's speech, language and communication needs

In addition to being able to recognise children's language needs, practitioners will also need to be have the knowledge and skill to begin the process of responding to these needs. Practitioners need to:

- have excellent observation and assessment skills;

- be skilled communicators;

- be aware of strategies to respond effectively to a child's speech, language and communication needs including: skilled communication; working with parents to enable them to support their child's learning; augmentative methods of communication such as signs and symbols);

- be aware of other professionals who can support children's language learning

Have excellent observation and assessment skills

Practitioners need to make effective, on-going assessments of children's abilities and needs. These observation and assessment processes should be well focused and effective to ensure that the process of identifying needs is accurate and timely. In these observations and assessments practitioners will need to use and apply knowledge of language learning and development to ensure that assessments accurately reflect the child's needs and abilities. This means that planned intervention can be well focused. The assessments also need to be timely so that intervention can begin as soon as possible because we know that early intervention has the greatest chance of success (Allen, 2011; Allen and Duncan Smith, 2008).

CASE STUDY

Assessing Raoul's needs

Four-year-old Raoul had been at nursery for a couple of months. Staff always allowed this time for the children to settle before they did a series of formal observations to get to know, and record, the children's abilities and needs.

The staff had been making informal observations of Raoul since he had come to nursery and, informally, had observed that his pattern of language and communication was unusual. Therefore, they decided to focus their observations on language to create a clear profile of his abilities and needs.

The staff undertook a series of observations over a week, observing Raoul in free play, at group times and during routines in the nursery. At the end of the week they met together and identified the patterns that they had observed in Raoul's language.

- *Overall he had quite sophisticated language use for his age but seemed to have difficulties with finding words.*

- *He spoke very, very quietly.*

- *He sometimes spoke through his teeth without moving his mouth.*

- *Sometimes he withdrew completely and wouldn't speak.*

- *When an adult asked him to repeat what he had said, as they hadn't heard him, he wouldn't speak.*

continued

CASE STUDY *continued*

- *He used pronouns inconsistently, for example, using both 'me' and 'you' when referring to himself.*

- *He repeated phrases he had heard in order to make a request; for example, he would say 'Do you want a drink' to mean 'I want a drink'.*

- *He would understand things in a literal way, for example, when the children were tidying up, a member of staff said, 'Come on, jump to it' and he had responded 'I don't want to jump' and another time a member of staff had dropped some paint and said 'Whoops, silly me, I'll have to pull my socks up' and Raoul had commented 'but you're not wearing any socks'.*

The staff agreed that some of the ways in which Raoul used language, for example, inconsistent use of pronouns, are quite typical at his age. However this combined with all the other aspects of his language that they had observed, and the frequency and persistence of the issues, led them to agree that they needed to seek further advice. They knew that they didn't have the necessary expertise to understand his needs sufficiently well to meet them in the nursery. They agreed that the teacher would speak with Raoul's dad when he came to pick him up to ask about their experiences of Raoul's talking at home and to ask for consent to seek further support.

Be a skilled communicator

Children learn language in social interactive contexts. The most important resource in children's language acquisition is other people. We know that interaction that involves meaningful, elaborated talk and communicative gesture, and that takes place within a literate environment, supports children's language acquisition (see Chapter 4). Practitioners working with young children need to be skilful communicators who are able to interact with children in the ways that we know support and enhance their language development. (Positive ways of interacting with children is covered in Chapter 7.)

The benefits of staff being skilled communicators are two-fold.

1. It can act as an intervention, once assessment has identified a child's language difficulties.

2. It can act as a preventative measure for children who need further support with acquiring language but are not yet experiencing identifiable difficulties. Children who have experienced a lack of stimulation to acquire and develop their language need skilled early input to enhance their language acquisition before difficulties occur.

Strategies to respond to children's needs

Skilful communication

The most important strategy in settings and schools is ensuring that staff are skilled in interacting with children in a way that is contingent on their abilities and needs. Strategies to achieve this are covered in Chapter 6.

Working with parents

Children learn their language in the communities in which they grow up. Schools and pre-school settings are one important part of that community. Parents and families also play a significant role in the development of children's language. Indeed, research shows that children's early language ability is linked to language that they are exposed to and involved in within their home (Hart and Risley, 1995). Therefore, working together with parents to support a child's language is vital in responding to children's language needs. The best outcomes for the child are likely when this takes place in a climate of good relationships and communication between setting/school and parents. This makes it easier to discuss concerns with parents, and to develop strategies to support the child's language that can be used in the home, the setting or the school. This cohesive approach is most likely to benefit the child.

CASE STUDY

Working with Charlie and his family

Observations of Charlie at his nursery school showed that, while his receptive language was good, he rarely spoke to the staff or the other children. When he did speak it was in very short sentences using only the bare minimum of words to communicate his needs. He almost never spoke to the staff or other children when engaged in play, and although he was attentive and observed other children's play he didn't attempt to join in or communicate with the other children. Charlie's key worker highlighted these concerns in discussions with other staff who agreed that Charlie's language development was likely to be affected by his lack of social interaction with others in the nursery.

Charlie's key worker spoke with Charlie's gran whom Charlie lived with. She explained that Charlie was very, very quiet at nursery and they wanted to encourage him to talk more with the staff and other children. She said that now she thought about it he was also very quiet at home, that they all lived very quietly as a family. The staff explained the importance of Charlie having the chance to talk and interact with others to acquire and develop his language skills. Charlie's gran was happy to help if she could. They asked her whether Charlie had any favourite toys or characters that they could use to encourage him to communicate more at nursery. Charlie's gran said that dinosaurs fascinated him. He loved to watch them on the TV and he carried one around with him at home. This gave the staff a very good starting point for planning some focused work with Charlie, both at nursery and at home.

Charlie's gran said that she would try and watch the dinosaur programmes with Charlie sometimes and talk to him about them. The nursery lent her some non-fiction books about dinosaurs and some storybooks with dinosaurs in them. She said that she would try to read them to him some nights when he was in bed. She would also encourage Charlie to tell her about the dinosaurs that he carried around with him.

The staff planned to use Charlie's interest to encourage him to interact more at nursery. They made sure that in their planning they included a range of activities based around dinosaurs, for example, small world play and dinosaur-based opportunities in art activities.

continued

CASE STUDY *continued*

Charlie's key worker would make sure that she encouraged Charlie to become involved in these activities and play with him. The staff also planned to turn the role-play area into a dinosaurs' cave. They decided to plan and make the cave with a group of children, including Charlie, using books, TV programmes and pictures to talk about what it would look like. Charlie's gran agreed to come in to nursery and join in with planning and making the cave, and bring some of Charlie's books and dinosaurs from home.

- *Why were observations important in meeting Charlie's needs?*

- *Why did staff approach Charlie's gran as one of the first things that they did?*

- *Why was it important to start from something that Charlie was interested in?*

- *What are the benefits of using an idea that comes from the home?*

- *How may the changes that Charlie's gran made at home support Charlie's language development?*

- *Why did Charlie's key worker make sure that she played with Charlie during the dinosaur activities?*

- *Why is involving Charlie's gran in the nursery activities a good idea in supporting Charlie's language development?*

Using augmentative methods of communication

Using augmentative methods of communication means using additional ways of communicating with a child alongside speech. This is important. Augmentative methods are not used to replace speech but to offer additional visual supports for spoken language through the use of signs and/or symbols.

Signs and symbols can be used in a number of ways including:

- to support *all* children's emerging speech – they provide an additional visual prompt for the words that are being used;

- to support children who are experiencing language difficulties – they provide an additional and different way of understanding the words that are being used;

- as a principal way of communication with children whose language and/or learning difficulties require them to have a different way of communicating.

Signs and symbols

The system of signs and symbols that we use is called Makaton. Makaton uses speech together with a sign (gesture) and/ or a symbol (picture), for example:

Sleep (gesture accompanying speech)

Sleep (picture)

Where? (Gesture accompanying speech)

Where? (Picture)

Figure 6.1: Makaton signs and symbols

Source: Adapted from www.makaton.org

With Makaton, signs are used with speech in spoken word order.

CASE STUDY

Using augmentative methods of communication in settings

Phoebe had taken over the leadership of Butts Lane playgroup. She had recently started working towards becoming an Early Years Professional and, as part of the process, was become increasingly aware of the number of children who came into the playgroup with speech, language and communication needs, and the setting's responsibility to meet these needs. She decided to start by focusing on the continuous provision. Alongside staff, Phoebe looked closely at the provision in the group and found many aspects of practice and provision that worked well.

- *Visual timetables were used to support routines for all children and enhance provision for children who needed additional support.*

- *The room was organised well each day with a wide range of activities that offered opportunities for interacting.*

- *A staff member used Makaton signs alongside speaking as a support to communication during child-initiated and adult-led activities and group times.*

- *They provided story sacks and a toy library for the children to borrow books and toys so that families could enjoy playing and reading together at home.*

The staff agreed that they could make their provision even better if:

- *the planning allowed for staff to have time to engage in focused and sustained talk with identified children at the activities that were on offer;*

- *more staff were able to use Makaton alongside speech to support the development of children's language and communication;*

- *the role-play themes were more carefully planned to encourage collaborative play and so offer more opportunities for the children to interact with one another and with staff – for example, a hairdresser's and a fancy-dress outfit shop;*

continued

CASE STUDY continued

- *symbols were used as visual prompts at group times more consistently – this would support all children's understanding of the expectations at group times.*

The staff agreed these changes and planned to implement them over the following three weeks. They also agreed a plan to review the children's progress with speech and communication in six-week blocks to make sure that their provision was meeting the children's ongoing needs. Phoebe also planned to contact outside support services to seek advice on what else they could do to support the children's speech, language and communication.

Be aware of other professionals who can support children's language learning

Once a child's speech, language and/or communication needs have been identified the initial focused support usually takes place in the setting or school, working in collaboration with parents. This focused support needs to be monitored so that staff know whether it is enabling identified children to make progress in acquiring and developing their language. For most children focused support that is contingent on their needs will enable them to make progress. However, for some children these interventions will not result in sufficient progress being made and they will continue to have difficulties. Staff will then, with parents' consent, need to seek the support of other professionals who can support children's language learning. This could be:

- a health visitor;

- a speech and language therapist;

- an educational psychologist;

- a paediatrician.

These other professionals can work with the child, their family and the school or setting. They will bring additional expertise to observe and assess the difficulties that a child is having, and to plan focused interventions to support the child's speech, language and communication needs.

SUMMARY

This chapter has explained what is meant by speech, language and communication needs. It has identified some of the reasons why children may have language difficulties and highlighted the fact that children who experience difficulties with their speech, language and/or communication are likely to face barriers to engaging in social interaction that builds relationships and enables learning. Early intervention is recognised as important in working with children who have language difficulties. How to respond to children with language difficulties is outlined, in particular the importance of having skilled practitioners who are able to interact with children in ways that enhance their language acquisition and development. The importance of observation and assessment to identify children's needs and working with children's families to support their language learning are discussed. Case studies illustrate how this can be achieved in settings.

FURTHER READING

Bowlby, J (1953) *Child Care and the Growth of Love*. London: Penguin.

Brice Heath, S (1983) *Ways with Words. Language, Life and Work in Communities and Classrooms*. New York: Cambridge University Press.

National Scientific Council on the Developing Child (2005) *Excessive Stress Disrupts the Architecture of the Developing Brain: Working Paper 3*. Available at: http://developingchild.harvard.edu/index.php/resources/reports_and_working_papers/working_papers/wp3/ (accessed 01.05.12)

Nutbrown, C, Hannon, P and Morgan, A (2005) *Early Literacy Work with Families*. London: SAGE

Purcell-Gates, V (1995) *Other People's Words. The Cycle of Low Literacy*. London: Harvard University Press.

Roulstone, S, Law, J, Rush, R, Clegg, J and Peters, T (2010) *Investigating the Role of Language in Children's Early Educational Outcomes*. Available at: www.education.gov.uk/publications/eOrderingDownload/DFE-RB134.pdf (accessed 29.02.12).

Snow, CE (2001) *The Centrality of Language: A Longitudinal Study of Language and Literacy Development in Low-income Children*. London: Institute of Education, University of London.

Part 2

Supporting children's language acquisition and development

7 Interaction to support language acquisition and development

This chapter enables you to understand:

- why it is important for early years practitioners to understand how to interact with young children;
- what strategies early years practitioners can use to support children's language acquisition and development;
- how to provide opportunities for talk and interaction;
- the importance of language play in children's language learning.

Introduction

Language is learned. We learn it from social interaction with the people around us. Almost all children are born with the potential to develop language and with a powerful drive to communicate with others. We, as adults, need to engage with this innate ability and powerful drive to communicate by providing opportunities for them to hear and use language. Indeed, young children are dependent upon the people around them to provide opportunities to engage with language in order to acquire and develop their own language skills. The evidence shows that the child's language ability is linked to the quality and quantity of language that they are exposed to and engage in as they learn (see Chapters 4 and 5).

Practitioners who work with young children need to be skilled in interacting with young children. They need to have a range of strategies that enable them to interact in ways that support and develop children's language acquisition.

Interaction that best supports children's language acquisition and development

Evidence suggests that elaborated talk (see Chapter 4) is most effective in supporting children's language acquisition. Put simply, this means that we need to say more than is necessary. At its most basic, talk can be used functionally – to ask for things, to protect ourselves, to issue requests and instructions, and this would probably be sufficient to function within society. But children who are learning language need more than this if they are going to develop their language to its full potential. They need to engage with people who talk communicatively as well as functionally – people who use language to explain, to discuss, to explore, to imagine, to express ideas and thoughts, who play with language though rhymes and jokes and wordplay; people who say more than is absolutely necessary.

Additionally, children need adults who listen carefully to them, who tune in and adapt their interaction to their abilities and needs, and who provide opportunities to engage in talking to practise and refine their developing language.

So, practitioners can best support children's language acquisition and development by:

• saying more than is necessary;

• listening carefully;

• providing opportunities for children to engage in talking.

Saying more than is necessary

Which strategies can practitioners use to ensure that they engage with children in ways that actively support and extend their language? What characterises interaction that goes beyond the functional and engages children in elaborated talk? How do practitioners ensure that they say more than is necessary?

Features of high quality adult child interaction in a nursery
Evidence shows that there are certain features of interaction with young children that best support their learning (Neaum, 2005).

One of the defining characteristics of positive interaction is *playfulness*; interaction in which practitioners clearly enjoy the processes of being engaged with the children in their talk and learning; where practitioners are lively and enthusiastic in their interactions with children.

Another characteristics is *commentary*. This means talking about the activity or experience as it is happening. The talk can be used to comment, explain, interpret or clarify. The important thing is that children are hearing language used to mediate their experience. Through commentary language is used to refer to a real experience in an authentic situation. Commentary can be used in a number of ways, such as:

• to articulate the observable processes in an experience or activity.

   For example, *I can see that you are...or...it's interesting how you....*

   In this way the child is given access to the language associated with the experience or activity, and to how we use language for thinking through the interpretation or explanation of what is happening;

• to reflect the child's learning and/or make links between what the child is learning now and prior learning.

   For example, *'Well done, you have worked out how to join that together. Can you remember last week when we were building the castle and needed to fix the big boxes together? We used sticky tape, but what you have done today fixes things together much more effectively.'*

In this way a child has access to language associated with the activity, and a model of how language can be used to link different aspects of activity and learning across time and space;

- to articulate the adult's thought processes while engaged in an activity or experience or just alongside a child.

For example, *'I was just wondering which book to read at storytime today. I love this one, but I think it is too long for my group so I'm going to look for a shorter one … one about animals I think, because it is our week to look after the rabbits so we've been talking about animals and what we need to do to look after them.'*

In this way children are exposed to language for thinking. They hear the thoughts that usually happen silently in our heads as we think things through. This broadens the range of language that they hear and models the way that we use language for thinking.

Teachable moments are moments when a practitioner notices that a child is ready to learn something and seizes the moment to teach the child, and so move the child's learning forward. It relies on the practitioner being able to notice and use moments as they arise to engage with the child to support their learning. Teachable moments can be used specifically to teach language, for example, vocabulary, or to model appropriate language usage or language for thinking, and to teach aspects of early literacy. Language is also likely to be part of most teaching exchanges and so, within each teachable moment, children are exposed to and engaged in social interaction which is likely to support their language learning alongside other aspects of their learning.

Scaffolding is a term coined by Bruner to explain the adult's role in supporting children's learning. He uses the image of the adult's provision and interaction acting like a scaffold that is built around the child while they are learning. Once the child has acquired the knowledge, skill or understanding the scaffold (adult support) can be removed. The scaffold is then put in place for the next stage of learning. Adults can scaffold children's talk by adopting interactive practices that encourage engagement in talk. Interactive strategies offer opportunities for the child to hear and respond to talk and for them to engage in interaction. These include:

- discussing;

- pondering;

- questioning;

- modelling;

- introducing relevant vocabulary.

All these strategies that scaffold and *extend* language learning require practitioners to engage in social interaction with children. At best, they require sustained interaction between adults and children which is likely to result in elaborated talk because using new vocabulary, pondering, discussing, questioning and modelling all require interaction in which the participants say more than is necessary.

Listening carefully

During activities practitioners need to be alert and sensitive to children's interests, abilities and needs. Interaction that engages children and results in elaborated talk needs to be enjoyable and of interest to the child. Therefore, to encourage sustained interaction practitioners need to listen carefully and engage with what interests the child. This may involve listening carefully so that provision has opportunities for play and learning based on a child's interests, or it may involve listening carefully and following the child's lead at times during interaction. Positive interaction with children (Neaum, 2005) is characterised by a sharing of the pace, timing and direction of interaction between adults and children so that both contribute to the understanding of the interaction, activity or experience; they construct their understandings together.

Additionally, listening carefully is important so that interaction is contingent on the child's current level of language ability and takes into account what knowledge and skill the child needs to develop next. By listening carefully practitioners can adjust their interaction to meet the child's language needs.

Evidence also suggests that when practitioners listen carefully and extend their talk with children it creates the opportunity for sustained shared thinking (Neaum, 2005). The EPPE study identified sustained shared thinking as a highly effective way of learning (Siraj-Blatchford et al., 2002:8). It requires that both adults and children listen carefully and communicate effectively to construct knowledge together.

DEFINITION

Sustained shared thinking: an episode in which two individuals work together in an intellectual way to solve a problem, clarify a concept, evaluate activities, extend a narrative, etc. Both parties must contribute to the thinking and it must develop and extend (Siraj-Blatchford et al., 2002:8).

ACTIVITY *1*

One of the best ways to become aware of how we communicate with children is to video ourselves talking with children and analyse the interaction.

Record yourself talking with children. You will need to record between five and ten minutes to get a good idea of your interaction.

Listen carefully to the recording. It may help to transcribe (write out) the interaction.

Analyse the interaction. Think about the following questions.

- *The tone of your voice – does it convey warmth and interest?*

- *How you speak – do you model good practice? What do you notice that is idiosyncratic to your way of talking? What impact do you think this has on the children?*

- *How quickly do you speak – is it at a pace that is appropriate to the children?*

continued

ACTIVITY *continued*

- *Do you listen? How do you demonstrate that you are listening?*

- *Waiting – do you give children time and space to respond in the interaction?*

- *Questions – what sort of questions do you ask? Open or closed? How many questions do you ask? Do the children have the chance to ask questions?*

- *What do you talk about and who decides the topics of conversation? Is it shared? Adult directed? Child directed? Do you contribute your own experiences and ideas? Do children have the opportunity to share their ideas and thoughts? How much is playful talk? How much management and direction? How much discussion and explanation? Do you use commentary? To what effect?*

- *Developing thought – do you ask for and give reasons and explanations? Do you encourage children to seek to understand and explain why? Do you allow them access to your ideas and thoughts through the use of commentary?*

- *How do you support children's language acquisition? How do you correct their errors? How do you introduce new vocabulary? How do you adapt your language to their needs?*

Once you have analysed your interaction you need to identify what you would like to change in your language use and interaction to enable you to best support children's language acquisition and development.

Further suggestions for analysing your interaction with children are available in the Every Child a Talker (ECAT) guidance.

Providing opportunities for children to engage in talking

For children to learn language they must use language as well as hear it (Saxton, 2010). Therefore, parents, carers and practitioners need to provide opportunities for children to use their emerging language, knowledge and skill. Clearly, children will need to have someone to talk with when engaged in their play so providing these opportunities has the benefit of enabling elaborated talk to happen; they require engagement in more talk than is necessary.

Talk in everyday routines

There are opportunities in all everyday routines to explain, discuss, comment and ask questions. Routines at home and in settings, such as shopping, preparing and eating food, tidying up, dressing, bathing and changing can involve a wide range of talk. What is important about the talk is that it involves more than management talk to get the task completed. It needs to involve talk that includes thoughts, ideas, explanations and reflections that the child is involved in and contributes to.

Providing opportunities for talk in settings

Settings need to plan their provision well to ensure that there are opportunities for the children to play and talk together with their peers and with practitioners. Careful thought about activities and experiences can create spaces and activities which strongly encourage children to communicate. For example:

- role-play that requires interaction, such as a barber or hairdresser's or a vet's practice or a fancy-dress shop;

- den building inside or out;

- large construction activities inside or out;

- using puppets;

- constructing water ways with tubes and piping.

Similarly, careful thought about how practitioners spend their time can provide opportunities for talk. It is important that the staff at activities are skilled in talking with young children and that it is clear to them that their task is to engage children in extended talk. Evidence suggests that the talk in settings and schools tends to focus predominantly on managing activities and children rather than sustaining conversation that results in learning (Tizard and Hughes, 1984). Therefore, time for staff to engage in sustained talk with children to support their language learning must be an important part of planning.

In addition to provision in the settings, practitioners need to consider how they can work with parents to help them to support their children's language learning. The REPEY study (Siraj-Blatchford et al., 2002) found that the best outcomes for children happen when settings support the ability of parents to provide a good home learning environment and don't just focus on meeting the adults' needs. This supports the view that what is important for young children's learning and development it is not who parents are, but what they do.

CASE STUDY

Providing opportunities for talk

Observational assessment of children in a Reception class identified that many of the children seemed to move quickly between activities, often on their own, which meant that they rarely engaged in a focused way at the activity and their conversations, with both staff and peers, tended to be quick and quite superficial. As a way of addressing this the staff decided that they would change their provision in two ways: firstly by providing more activities that required the children to engage and talk with staff and one another; and secondly by ensuring that the staff organisation enabled staff to be at activities to play and talk with the children.

The first task was to change the role-play into a barber's and hairdresser's.

They decided to do this with the children so that they could use the setting up of the role-play area as an opportunity to engage in focused activity and talk with the children.

continued

- First thing in the morning they read a story about visiting the barber and discussed what happens there, and the differences between a barber and a hairdresser.

- The children then discussed and made a list of the things that they would need to create a barber's shop and hairdresser's in the classroom. The teacher wrote the list, modelling writing for the children.

- The children were given a short list of items to collect from round the nursery. The list had the word and a picture of the equipment and the children had to tick it off as they found it. They completed this activity in pairs.

- Together as a group the children gathered all the equipment that they had and crossed it off the main list – this left a few items.

- The group then went together to the local shops to buy the last few items.

- Once back in the classroom some of the group, with a practitioner, constructed the shop entrance from large construction equipment; others, again with a practitioner, made the signs and price lists to go in the area.

- The children then put all the equipment in the barber's and hairdresser's and put up the signs.

- The group were given half an hour to play in the area to check that everything was available.

- The children were then asked to pair up with a child in the class who hadn't been involved in setting up the role-play area and show them around the area before it opened – to explain what the equipment was, how it can be used, how the appointment system worked and show them the prices.

- The shops opened on the following day.

Read through the case study.

- Identify where, to make the activity successful, children would need to be: engaged in talking with their peers and/or engaged in talking with staff.

- Why are activities that require communication between children and practitioners important for children's language learning?

- Why is it important that staff plan these activities for young children?

- Why is it important that staff get involved in the activities and engage in talking with the children?

- List some other examples of activities or experiences that require children to talk with their peers and with staff and so practise, adapt and refine their language.

Creating spaces in settings to develop speaking and listening

Elizabeth Jarman (2007) has developed some interesting work on creating 'communication-friendly spaces' in settings. It flows from observation of learning spaces for young children in other countries such as Denmark and Sweden. She argues that the space in a setting can be organised in ways that encourage children to talk and listen and so support the development of their language and communication. Speaking and listening, she argues, are encouraged by creating 'communication-friendly spaces' within settings. There are a number of features of these spaces. These include:

- a lack of extraneous stimulus – practitioners are encouraged to create a calm environment through the use of muted natural colours for displays and resources, uncluttered wall and tabletop displays and well-organised, readily available resources;

- as much natural light as possible;

- gentle lighting where lighting is needed, such as the use of fairy lights;

- low levels of background noise;

- the creation of enclosed 'den-like' areas inside and outside that provide spaces for children to go to talk, read and play;

- the creation of spaces that are specifically for talking and listening, such as a storytelling chair.

ACTIVITY 3

Look at the list of features of communication-friendly spaces (above).

- *Compare these features with your experience of play spaces for young children, for example, in nurseries, playgroups, in the home.*

- *What changes need to be made to spaces you have seen to create places that encourage children to acquire, use and develop their language?*

- *Think about your own work and home environment. Which spaces are most conducive to being calm, interacting well and working effectively?*

- *How does this map to what Jarman is suggesting for spaces for children's learning?*

- *What is your view about Jarman's ideas?*

These spaces are one way of encouraging children to engage in speaking and listening in the setting. However, 'communication-friendly spaces' will not support children's language development in themselves; they will only have an impact on children's language development if children are engaged in play and talk with their peers and practitioners. As we know, children's language development requires that they have opportunities to use, practice, adapt and refine their language knowledge and skills.

The importance of language play in children's language learning

Language play means exactly what it says: playing around with language in rhymes, jokes, sound and wordplay, imitation, using different voices, and all other playful ways of using language.The term often used for this is 'ludic'. The term derives from the Latin *ludus*, meaning 'play', and is an adjective meaning playful.

As adults we play around with language. We bend and break language rules and create new, different playful meanings from words and phrases. It is an important part of our social interaction and it is done for fun! Crystal (1998) identifies a whole range of ways in which we, as adults, play with language, for example, puns, jokes, use of dialect words and phrases, nonsense words, creating new meanings for words, limericks, using tone of voice, pitch, speed, rhythm, to alter words and meanings.

Children also play with language as they are acquiring, developing and refining their language knowledge and skill. They seem to be drawn to sound play, word play, imitation, rhyme and absurdity in language. Observe young children and see that they seem to enjoy the sounds and effect of playing around with language, almost for its own sake; rhymes don't have to make sense, strings of rhyming words are created just to say them, jokes are made up that aren't funny to a wider audience, they're delighted by 'naughty' words and by nonsense words, and find it hilarious when people get words wrong.

The benefits of language play

Language play is good for children's language acquisition and development, and therefore we should strongly encourage, and even join in, their language play. However, language play needs ownership by the children. If language play becomes another pedagogical tool for adults to use to deliver outcomes it loses its very essence: that of spontaneity. Children need to be able to delight in the creativity and immediacy of language play, to indulge and develop the things that appeal to them, to say silly things and make themselves giggle, to have control over the pace, timing, direction and flow of the language play; and not have it taken over by adults. When children are allowed to develop their language play a range of benefits flow from this play (Crystal, 1998).

Language play helps children learn language. Crystal (1998) cites the work of Piaget and Bruner who suggest that children play with the skills that they are in the process of acquiring: play-as-practice. As young children are in the process of acquiring language it follows that this language play is a way of using, understanding and refining their language knowledge and skill.

- *It aids pronunciation* through a focus on the properties of sound, particularly rhyming sounds.

- *It helps with the acquisition of grammar* through the focus on riddles, jokes and wordplay – children begin to understand some things about the structure of a language.

- *It supports semantic development* because play with words, puns, nonsense words and nonsense talk develops an understanding of the meanings of words, phrases and sentences.

- *This all supports the learning of conversational skills:* all the skills above are needed for effective interaction with others.

Language play contributes to metalinguistic development. Meta-linguistic development is the ability to understand and talk about the properties of language – having a language for language. This requires us to stand outside of the language, to observe and evaluate it and have a language for talking about this. Evidence shows that this is an important skill when learning to read and write (Sulzby and Teale, 1991). Language play requires very similar skills: it requires a certain level of awareness about language to enable us to deviate from what we know as 'normal' language. Therefore we need to be able to stand back from language and see how it works to enable us to shape it differently for our enjoyment.

Language play is a precursor to later verbal skill in poetry, rhetoric and other forms of eloquence (Sanches and Kirshenblatt-Gimblett,1976). Poetry, rhetoric and eloquence can be seen as forms of wordplay. Early wordplay that engages with a delight in the complexities and nuances of language can act as a starting point for the development of these adult 'verbal arts'.

Enabling language play

Practitioners need to encourage children's language play. This may mean leaving children to engage in play without intervention, allowing them the freedom to create and develop language games and wordplay. It may also mean engaging in the children's language games, taking the cues from them and allowing the pace, timing, direction and flow of the interaction to be led by the children. In particular, it is important that practitioners (and parents) don't take a view that it is all 'silly talk' and intervene to stop children developing and indulging their play.

Practitioners may also use some of the language play that children are interested in to shape their provision and interaction. Firstly, they can do this by demonstrating enjoyment in language play, by engaging with the children's ideas and by demonstrating our own interest and enjoyment in words and language. Additionally, they can provide opportunities for children to engage with language play, for example, provide and read nonsense books and poems, use riddles and rhymes in activities and create nonsense words and ideas, perhaps as starting points to activities.

CASE STUDY

Creaturmals: a cross between a creature and an animal

The nursery was doing a topic on animals. One of the activities was 'Create a creaturmal', a new, never-before-seen animal, a cross between two or three animals'. The idea came from observing children in the nursery playing with their names, joining together two names of people who were friends to create one name. They had been doing this for a while and some of them were now trying to combine three names.

continued

CASE STUDY *continued*

The idea of a creaturmal was introduced by a series of pictures that staff had made that combined two animals. The children were asked to think about names for the animals over the next few days.

Over the following week the children created their own creaturmal and worked out its name, what it ate and where it lived. Some of the children decided that everything about the creaturmal had to be a combination of words, so what they ate, where they lived and what their babies were called were all created through word and language play. Some children chose to represent their creaturmal in their art work and role-play and label it with the new words that they had created.

- *How did the teachers use and adapt the children's language play?*

- *How did they ensure that they allowed the children to retain ownership of the word-play idea?*

- *How did the children develop and adapt the activity in line with their interests in words and language?*

- *What do you think children learned from this language play?*

- *Why is it important that the teachers allowed the children freedom to develop their own ideas within the activity?*

SUMMARY

This chapter has considered why it is important for practitioners to know how to interact effectively with young children. It has outlined a number of strategies that have been shown to support children's language learning, namely, saying more than is necessary, listening carefully and providing opportunities for children to talk. Ways in which practitioners can provide opportunities for children's talk have been described. The importance of language play in supporting language acquisition and development has been discussed and ways in which practitioners can engage with children in their language play outlined.

FURTHER READING

Crystal, D (1998) *Language Play*. London: Penguin.

Siraj-Blatchford, I, Sylva, K, Muttock, S, Gilden, R and Bell, D (2002) Researching Effective Pedagogy in the Early Years. Research Report RR356, DCFS. Available at www.327matters.org/Docs/RR356.pdf (accessed 02.05.12)

Sulzby and Teale (1991) Emergent Literacy, in Barr, R, Kamil, M, Mosenthal, P and Pearson, PD *Handbook of Reading Research*. Volume 2. New Jersey: Lawrence Earlbaum.

Sylva, K, Meluish, E, Sammons, P, Siraj Blatchford, I, Taggart, B and Elliot, K (2003) Effective Provision of Pre-School (EPPE) Project: Findings from the Pre-School Period. Available at: http://eppe.ioe.ac.uk/eppe/eppefindings.htm (accessed 02.05.12)

8 Supporting bilingual and multilingual children's language learning

This chapter enables you to understand:

- what is meant by bilingualism and multilingualism;
- the reasons why we need to value and respect children's first (or home) language(s);
- the benefits of being bilingual or multilingual;
- the observable stages in learning English as an additional language;
- strategies to support bilingual and multilingual children's language learning.

Introduction

Children are born into families and communities which all use language (spoken and/or signed). They acquire and develop their language knowledge and skill in this family and community. This means that children who grow up in families and communities in which there is more than one language spoken will acquire and develop the languages that they hear and use to communicate with people in their community. Many children growing up in the UK live in a community in which different languages are spoken. These children will either grow up, or become, bilingual or multilingual.

Most children who speak more than one language will use different languages in different contexts, for example, one language at home, one at school. Once this is established children will comfortably switch between languages according to context.

What is meant by bilingualism and multilingualism?

Children who are bilingual live in two languages. Children who are multilingual live in more than two languages. This means that these children need to use more than one language to interact in their normal daily life in their family, school and community.

Some bilingual and multilingual children will learn English from birth alongside their home and community language(s) and so start in settings and/or schools speaking both languages. Other children will learn and speak only their home and community language(s) at home and learn English when they come to nursery or school. Other children will come to live in the UK after they have learned their home and community language(s) in another country. These children may be in England temporarily accompanying parents working or studying here, or be refugees, or have come to live here permanently. These children will need to learn English when they start school in the UK to enable them to form and maintain friendships and to learn. In some countries there are two official languages so the whole country operates bilingually. For example, in Wales there are two official languages, Welsh and English. Both languages have equal status in law, so everything is provided and translated into both languages. This means that many children in Wales grow up living in two languages.

DEFINITION

Bilingual: living in two languages.

Multilingual: living in more than two languages.

Why is it important that we support children's home language(s)?

There can be little doubt that children who are at school in the UK need to know or learn English to access all that settings and schools offer. However, this focus on the need for children to acquire English has, in the past, obscured the importance of valuing and supporting other language(s) that are spoken in homes and communities. This has begun to change and it is now recognised that, for children who speak languages other than English, English needs to be added to their repertoire of languages rather than home and community languages being replaced by English. There are a number of reasons why we must recognise and value children's first or home language(s) alongside supporting their acquisition of English.

A question of rights

We are signatories to the United Nations Convention on the Rights of the Child. This convention enshrines in law a series of rights that signatories have agreed are worthy aspirations for all people and have agreed to support in their country. Article 30 states:

> *In those States in which ethnic, religious or linguistic minorities or persons of indigenous origin exist, a child belonging to such a minority or who is indigenous shall not be denied the right, in community with other members of his or her group, to enjoy his or her own culture, to profess and practice his or her own religion, or to use his or her own language.*

People who speak more than one language therefore have the right to use and maintain their home language(s). Our national laws (and perhaps more importantly our ways of being) must therefore reflect our commitment to supporting these rights in our country. As part of this we need, in schools and settings, to recognise and actively value children's use of their home and community languages alongside learning English.

Language is a significant part of a child's identity

Our relationships, our understandings and our ways of being are all mediated through language. It is, in large part, through language spoken at home and in our communities that we come to know and understand ourselves as part of a family, a community and a culture, through which we develop our cultural identity and cultural knowledge. This cultural knowledge and identity is who the child is, and how settings and schools respond to this is vital to the child's sense of self. In 1975 the Bullock Report recognised that for many children their experience of schooling was one of having to deny their cultural knowledge and identity and live as if school and home were completely separate worlds. This has changed in the current stated aims in statutory curricula documentation, for example, in the Early Years Foundation Stage which has four guiding principles that acknowledge difference and diversity, (although some would argue that for many children little has actually changed). So, in terms of language, as language is an integral part of identity, by recognising and valuing children's home and community language(s) we support and enhance their developing sense of self.

Starting from the child

The very best starting point for all aspects of children's learning, including language learning, is their current level of learning; building on what they already know and can do. Most children who speak one or more languages other than English in their homes and communities will come to settings and schools competent in language. It is important that we as practitioners recognise this competence in our provision and offer children meaningful, rather then tokenistic, opportunities to use their language(s) alongside learning English. Similarly, it is important that we recognise that most bilingual and multilingual children are very competent language users and take this as the starting point in our interactions, assessments and resulting provision. In doing this we enact our commitment to recognising and valuing children's first language.

In addition to questions of rights and identity, supporting and valuing children's home language, so that it continues to develop as a child acquires English, has both benefits for a child's acquisition of English and wider linguistic and cognitive benefits. These benefits will be outlined in detail below, however it is important that, as Dury and Robertson (2008) observe, practitioners recognise first and foremost the innate cultural and social value in bilingualism and multilingualism rather than see the benefits purely in terms of how bilingualism and multilingualism act as a support for learning English.

The benefits of being bilingual or multilingual

Language binds us all to particular places, people, communities, histories, stories, songs, myths and a wide range of cultural and social practices (Whitehead, 2010). Children who have access to more than one language also have access to a rich and diverse range of human experience. Living in more than one language potentially offers children first-hand experience and understanding about language, societies and cultures.

Similarly, being bilingual or multilingual hugely extends language capacity, both language for communication and language for thinking. To be able to use different languages brings a wider capacity for understanding and expressing thoughts and ideas, the potential for a more nuanced vocabulary, and it enables different ways of interacting and communicating across societies and cultures. Additionally, as children grow and learn and become literate, an extended language capacity enables access to a range of literature and other texts in their original language. Without doubt this extended language capacity has significant potential benefits, across all aspects of life and learning, for both the child and the wider community in which they grow and learn.

Being bilingual or multilingual has been shown to enhance metalinguistic awareness: an awareness of, and knowledge about, language. This is because children who are learning more than one language have the advantage of becoming aware of their language and thinking as they use, adapt and accommodate language in their interactions. At its simplest, the use of one or more languages enables children to develop their understanding of the concept of words and language. Bilingual and multilingual children use different words and language in different contexts for the same thing, for example, having two or more words for an object or an action used with different people in different contexts. This code switching heightens an awareness of words and language.

Additionally, all of us accommodate our language to the audience and context. We alter how we speak according to whom we are speaking. We make changes to the language we use and how we speak (for example, the pace, tone, register) according to socially expected patterns of interaction. Children who are learning more than one language do this on a greater scale and in a more complex way. Bilingual and multilingual children learn the style shifts within each of the languages that they speak as they move between languages. This ability to differentiate their language use and style shift across more than one language also heightens children's awareness and sensitivity to language. The ability to be aware and alive to language develops metalinguistic awareness, which in turn has a positive effect on later language and literacy learning.

DEFINITION

Two terms from linguistics which describe ways in which we adapt our language.

Code shifting: switching between languages.

Style shifting: making changes according to audience and context *within* a language.

Becoming bilingual and multilingual: children learning English as an Additional Language

There are recognised stages of additional language learning (Tabors, 1997). It is important that practitioners are aware of these stages so that they can match their expectations, interaction and provision to the child's needs.

1. Children use their home language
   Children coming into an environment in which a different language is spoken may use their home language initially with the expectation that they will be understood. This period is likely to be quite brief as children realise that they are not understood. The

messages that they receive about the value of the their home language are very important at this stage – it is important that their home language is valued and that they don't begin to believe that they must replace their home language with English; rather that learning English will add to their repertoire of languages.

2. A silent or non-verbal stage

Many bilingual and multilingual children on entering an unfamiliar early years setting will go through a period when they don't interact verbally. They often continue to interact non-verbally (facial expressions such as smiles and gestures such as pointing) and spend time watching and listening intently to tune into the language around them. At this stage children can be observed using English quietly to themselves – rehearsing the language that they are acquiring.

At this stage practitioners need to:

- keep talking, even when children don't respond;

- accept non-verbal responses;

- praise all efforts, however minimal, at verbal communication;

- use clear, precise language spoken at a normal pace, pitch and volume so that children begin to develop an ear for the sound of natural spoken English;

- interact in ways that encourage children to repeat words (or numbers);

- actively include children in group activities and experiences where they are hearing and responding to language.

3. Beginning to use English

Children begin to use single words, formulaic phrases and repetition during the earliest stages of learning English. Children often learn and use 'chunks' of language that they have heard, for example, parts of rhymes or songs, routine greetings or language used at specific times such as group times or registration.

4. Producing and using English

With practice from opportunities to hear and use English children will eventually begin to produce more complex language by building on and extending the 'chunks' of language that they are using. This may start by use of single words or 'chunks' strung together to approximate to the intended meaning. Children need ongoing opportunities to hear English and appropriate opportunities to use their developing language to support this process of language learning.

(Tabors, 1997)

It is important to be aware that these developmental patterns, like all developmental patterns, are guides only. Children will develop at their own pace and this will be dependent upon a range of factors. The pace of development will vary between children, for example, one child may spend a lot of time watching and listening before very quickly moving into speaking in complete sentences, another child may very quickly start using single words and stay at this stage for a long time. Additionally, the stages themselves are not discrete. Children are likely to move backwards and forwards between the stages depending on the context. They may also be operating at one or more stages at the same time according to the context in which they are using English. As practitioners it is important that we observe children closely so that we are aware of children's changing abilities and needs and match our provision and interaction to those abilities and needs.

CASE STUDY

Observing Ludwika learning English

Ludwika enters the nursery holding her mother's hand. She goes over to the art and craft area and stands watching a nursery nurse organising a hand painting activity at the painting table. The children are each making hand printed cards for Mother's Day. Ludwika takes a turn at the activity in silence, except for the correct one-word response to questions about the colour of the paint and the card: 'What's that colour?' 'Yellow'. Ludwika then moves onto the carpet where children are playing with a wooden train set, solid shapes and small construction materials. She is silent while she plays on her own. After a few minutes, another child takes one of her shapes and she protests 'No, mine, not yours. Look.' There is no response and she continues playing. Talk is going on around her, but it is not addressed to Ludwika. The nursery teacher walks past the carpet and Ludwika attracts her attention, 'Mr Ashley, look.' The teacher looks, smiles and walks away. Then it is tidy-up time. Ludwika sits with the teacher in a group of seven children for small group time. The focus is the song 'Heads, shoulders, knees and toes' and playing a game to teach the parts of the body. She joins in the refrain of the song 'Knees and toes', listens, watches attentively and participates mainly non-verbally during the game. Then the teacher directs the children: 'It's time to go out in the garden'. She finds Ludwika sitting on her own singing to herself 'knees and toes, knees and toes', before she goes out to play.

(Adapted from Dury and Roberstson, 2008)

Read through the case study.

- *What stage of English acquisition is Ludwika at? Find examples to support your assessment.*

- *Notice how the teacher interacted with Ludwika. What more could he have done to support Ludwika's language learning?*

- *Why do you think singing supports bilingual children's language learning?*

- *What should the staff do to support Ludwika in her next steps of learning?*

Strategies to support bilingual and multilingual children's language learning

The language needs of children who arrive in early years settings speaking language(s) other then English are two-fold:

1. to know that their first language is valued, and have the opportunity to use it at times in their play and interactions;

2. to learn English.

There are a number of ways in which practitioners in settings can support both these aspects of children's language learning. The first is to value the child's first language so, where possible, use this language both in setting provision, through links to home-based activities and talk, and as a bridge to learning English. This can be done by:

- ensuring that provision reflects diversity of language and cultural heritage – this should be evident across all aspects of provision, books, play equipment, displays and in *all* children learning greetings and simple words in different languages;

- making good links with children's home and community and using community knowledge and resources to include activities and experiences that use children's home language and culture in the setting. A significant benefit of this, alongside the enrichment of the learning for all children, is that the bilingual or multilingual child is in the position of being knowledgeable and competent – which will inevitably have a positive effect on their sense of self;

- enabling parents and community members to become involved in school-type activities at home using the child's first language, for example, clay and dough, puppets, small world play or block-play. This may involve creating a library of play sacks for children to borrow and take home;

- using bilingual staff members to support children's first language learning and their learning of English. Bilingual staff can provide a bridge between the children's languages as they add English to their repertoire of languages.

Other ways of supporting both aspects of language learning are as follows.

- Use visual cues across activities and provision.

- Allow children plenty of time to 'stand-and-stare'. Time to watch and listen, to take in what is happening in the setting and get used to the sound of spoken English is invaluable.

- Allow children space and time to try out their new language. Expect that they will need time to rehearse what they know and can say before they are able to become actively involved in an activity that requires them to speak.

- Provide rich and frequent opportunities for children to hear English.

- Provide frequent and developmentally appropriate opportunities for children to use their emerging English. This requires that a precise assessment of the child's abilities and needs has been made so that interaction is appropriate to the child's needs as a bilingual or multilingual child's ability may not be reflected in their English language capability.

ACTIVITY 1

Describe how you would provide for the needs of bilingual and/or multilingual children in these typical nursery activities:

- *role-play;*

- *storytime;*

- *dressing-up;*

- *weaving;*

- *drink and snack time.*

Use the list of strategies to support bilingual and multilingual children's language learning outlined above to inform your ideas.

In what ways would you change what you do and what you provide as children become increasingly proficient in English to ensure that the provision remained aligned with the children's needs?

SUMMARY

This chapter has outlined what is meant by bilingualism and multilingualism. A range of benefits of speaking more than one language are identified, including an increased understanding about language, societies and cultures and an extended language capacity for language for communicating and thinking.

The importance of valuing a child's first or home language has been discussed as an issue of rights, identity and good practice. Observable stages in learning English as an Additional Language have been identified and strategies to support bilingual and multilingual children's language learning outlined.

FURTHER READING

Baker, C (2011) *Foundations of Bilingual Education and Bilingualism*, 5th edition. Bristol: Multilingual Matters.

Bialystok, E (2001) *Bilingualism in Development: Language, Literacy and Cognition*. Cambridge: Cambridge University Press.

Bilingual Research Journal

Cunningham-Anderson, U and Anderssan, S (2004) *Growing Up With Two Languages. A Practical Guide*. London: Routledge.

International Journal of Bilingual Education and Bilingualism

Li Wei (2006) *The Bilingualism Reader*. London: Routledge.

Robertson, LH (2002) Parallel literacy classes and hidden strengths: learning to read in English, Urdu and classical Arabic. *Reading, Literacy and Language (UKRA)*, November, 36 (3): 119–126.

Tabors, P (1997) *One Child, Two Languages: A Guide for Preschool Educators of Children Learning English as a Second Language*. Baltimore: Paul Brookes Publishing.

The Bullock Report (1975) *A Language for Life*. Available at: www.educationengland.org.uk/documents/bullock/ (accessed 15.02.12)

United Nations Convention on the Rights of the Child. Available at: www.unicef.org/crc/ (accessed 05.02.12)

WEBSITES

www.bilingualism-matters.org.uk

www.bilingualism.bangor.ac.uk

9 Starting from the child

This chapter enables you to understand:

- what we mean by starting from the child;
- the importance of observation and assessment in enabling provision and interaction to start from the child;
- how to use popular culture as the starting point for supporting children's language acquisition and development.

Introduction

Imagine that you were going away on holiday. How would you work out what you needed to buy for the holiday? Imagine that you are going to going to the gym. You grab your gym bag and look in it. How do you work out what else you need to put in the bag? Imagine that you were going to decorate a room. You don't have your own equipment so you borrow a friend's box of decorating equipment. How would you know what else you needed?

ACTIVITY 1

Let's take a closer look at one of these scenarios.

Imagine that you were going to decorate your bedroom. You want to put wallpaper on one wall and paint the other three walls and all the woodwork. You don't have your own equipment so you borrow a friend's box of decorating equipment. Your friend brings the box to your house and you open the box.

- *What would you do on opening the box?*

- *Why would you do this? What information would this give you?*

- *How would this affect what you do next?*

- *Why is looking in the box a good starting point for planning your decorating task?*

- *What are the links between this process and working with children to find out what activities and experiences are relevant for them to learn?*

In all these scenarios, to manage the situation effectively, you would need to make an assessment of what was already there. This would inform you about what else is needed and then this information would be the starting point for what you do next.

The same processes can be used when working with people. Imagine a family worker. In order to work effectively with the family the family worker would need to:

• establish what the current situation is;

• from this, work out what is needed;

• use this information to plan what to do next.

This pattern of assessment of the current level of learning, the identification of abilities and needs and planning of next steps is an important aspect of an early years practitioner's professional role.

What is meant by starting from the child?

Starting from the child means using the child's level of learning, understanding, skills and interests as the starting point for provision and interaction. It means that you look at the child first and use this information to decide what comes next to enable their learning. It is the opposite of looking at documents, curriculum guidance or learning outcomes as your starting point and planning provision to teach what they specify without regard to the abilities and needs of the children in front of you.

This pattern of provision is applicable to all areas of learning including language acquisition and development and becoming literate. Starting from the child requires that practitioners have an excellent understanding of all aspects of language learning, including how children learn to talk and how they become literate. This knowledge and understanding will enable practitioners to:

• make precise, detailed assessments of children's current levels of learning and know what they are engaged and interested in;

• have a clear understanding of what comes next in their learning;

• know how to provide opportunities for that learning.

Using observation to start from the child

Detailed and precise observation-based assessments of children's learning and interests should provide the starting point for provision and interaction. This, of course, means that within any group of children there will be a range of needs, abilities and interests. This required breadth of provision can be achieved in early years through careful, focused planning of both child and adult-initiated play and activities.

Observing children provides the necessary information for starting from the child. It enables us to:

• understand what individual children know and can do;

• understand what individual children are interested in and how they learn best so that we can support their learning and development effectively;

- support overall planning and provision;

- match our approaches and interactive strategies to children's needs to best support their learning and development;

- further develop our understanding of how children learn, linking theory with practice.

An important part of understanding starting points for providing for children's learning is to observe what they are interested in. Where do they play? What do they play? Who do they play with? Which activities, experiences or themes engage them? Interest is an excellent motivator for children. When children are engaged in an activity or experience that is absorbing they are more likely to learn. We can use the information we gather through observation to inform what we do and what we provide to ensure that we reflect children's interests in our provision.

Another important question to ask is: how do children learn best? This will be different for different children. Children will have a preferred way to explore their world; it might be alongside other children or alongside an adult; it may be in group work or on their own; it might be by returning over and over again to an activity; it might be with a singular focus on an activity; it might be working with the same schema through a variety of different activities and experiences. Through observation, practitioners need to become aware of individual children's preferences and, as with all other aspects of observation, ensure that provision starts from close knowledge of individual children in the group.

When observation and assessment of children's play is carried out effectively it is done with compassion, recognising that the aim of observing children's learning is to see a child as an individual with strengths and needs. If we are committed to starting from the child it is important that we are aware that all children will come into settings with different experiences. These experiences will have had a direct impact on their learning. For some children their experiences will have supported their learning and development and they will have knowledge skills and aptitudes that enable them to access school-based learning easily. Other children's experiences will mean that we need to provide time and opportunity for them to develop and learn in order to access school-based learning. Observation that informs provision and interaction is known as formative assessment. This is in contrast to summative assessment which summarises learning at a given point in time.

DEFINITION

Formative assessment: assessment focused on producing information that is used to adapt provision to meet a child's needs. This is often referred to as 'assessment for learning'.

Summative assessment: assessment focused on summarising a child's learning and development at a particular point in time. This is often referred to as 'assessment of learning'.

It is also important to be aware that, as practitioners, we make choices about what we observe and to realise that these choices indicate what we value in children and children's play. It is almost always practitioners who select what to observe, when to observe and where to observe children's learning, and we bring to that situation many assumptions about what is worthwhile to observe. It is important therefore that we are aware of what assumptions and prejudices we hold about what constitutes worthwhile play, worthwhile activities and worthwhile interests and how this impacts on what, how and when we observe children. Where necessary we need to challenge these assumptions within ourselves and others to ensure that our observations of children reflect all of who they are and so enable us to make clear assessments of appropriate starting points for provision and interaction.

We may also find ourselves only observing the easily observable, for example, what children say and do. This is clearly an important part of observation but other aspects of who children are are equally important: their feelings, thoughts, attitudes and dispositions. How do we observe these? How do we ensure that our assessment of who children are and what they can do is holistic so that we are confident that we are starting from the child's needs and interests? One way of achieving this is multidimensional observation, both content and perspective. In this way we ensure that our assessments of children have breadth as well as depth and reflect the complexity of young children's learning, interests and experiences. For example, practitioners may use the mosaic approach (Clark and Moss, 2001) alongside a more traditional pattern of observation in order to include the child's perspective on themselves, their world and their learning. These combined approaches are likely to enable us to have a more holistic understanding of children to inform our starting points for provision and interaction.

THEORY FOCUS

The mosaic approach to observing children's learning (Clark and Moss, 2001)

The mosaic approach is a multi-method approach to bringing together children's own views of their lives and their pre-setting. It aims for children to be participants in constructing an understanding of their lives. The approach uses a range of ways of 'listening' to children to construct this understanding of their lives.

- Observation
  Children are listened to through observation based upon two questions: *What is it like to be here?* and *Do you listen to me?*

- Discussion (child conferencing) with the child
  This is based on a framework of 14 questions around the key themes of: why children came to nursery; the role of adults; favourite and worst activities and people.

- The use of:
  cameras – children take photographs of things that are important to them in the setting;
  tours – a tour of the setting led by the child, again highlighting the things that are important to the child;
  mapping – in discussion with the staff, children use their photographs and aspects of the tour to record their views of the setting.

Starting from the child

Staff had noticed how Dr Who had become the theme of play for a group of boys. They thought that this interest would be good to develop to support the boys' language learning and beginning literacy.

Initially, the staff decided to complete some focused observations on the boys to make sure that their profiles accurately reflected the boys' abilities in language and literacy learning.

Once this was completed the staff brought this information to the planning meeting to inform their plans. The boys had a range of abilities and needs. Some of them needed opportunities to talk and practise, adapt and refine their spoken language; others were very competent linguistically and were beginning to engage with emergent reading and writing activities. They agreed that they would use the theme of Dr Who to provide opportunities for interaction and emergent literacy.

This information both about the boys' interest and their levels of learning provided the starting point for the provision.

- *Initially, the staff watched a favourite episode of* Dr Who *with the children who wanted to watch and looked at some* Dr Who *annuals. These were then used as a reference to plan and design an initial role-play Tardis with the children. Different episodes and books were introduced over the following weeks to change and adapt the role-play area to maintain the children's interest.*

- *Opportunities for discussion and modelled reading and writing were included in the planning of the Tardis role-play area and making of the outfits.*

- *Opportunities to encourage talk and interaction were included in the Tardis; two-way radios, tape recorders to record star logs, joint control areas.*

- *Opportunities for emergent literacy were included in the form of labels on the controls, instructions on how to use the equipment, charts to record journeys, log books to complete, and a gallery area for the children to (according to their ability) draw, label or write about the aliens they had encountered.*

- *Staff observed the adventures that the children were creating in the area and, in small groups, drew the adventures as a story board. With some of the children they then recorded the story for other children to listen to.*

- *Each day staff played in the area alongside the children with a clear focus on engaging with a particular child or children to support their language and/or literacy learning. The initial assessments provided the information for this focused work.*

In these ways the staff used the starting point of the boys' interest and levels of learning to involve them in language and literacy activities. The boys were interested and engaged and the provision was at an appropriate level for them to practise and refine the skills that they had and to move forward in their learning.

Using popular culture as a starting point for supporting children's language learning

One of the ways in which we can start from the child is by engaging with their interests beyond the setting. Very young children are familiar with a whole range of texts and artefacts based, predominantly, on media characters from TV, films and games. This knowledge and enthusiasm for popular culture can be used to inform what we provide in settings. Popular culture refers to the use of texts, artefacts and practices that appeal to large numbers of children and which are often mass-produced. It is often related to TV, film or book characters. It is evident in a range of media and materials in children's lives.

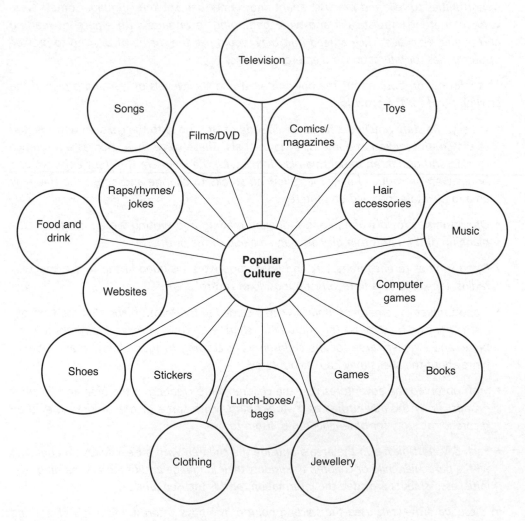

Figure 9.1: Expressions of children's popular culture
Source: Adapted from Marsh and Millard, 2000.

Traditionally popular culture, in the form of books, games, DVDs and artefacts, has been part of children's lives outside settings and schools. Provision in settings and schools has, in contrast, been informed by a particular body of ideas and literature, often referred to as a canon.

DEFINITION

Canon: a standard set of works. Often used to refer to a group of literary works that are considered important. A validity or authority is afforded to the work within a canon. There are no rigid criteria for inclusion in a literary canon; those who make the decisions are literary critics, scholars, teachers and others who inform curriculum content. This is often through comment, choice and usage rather than any formal process. Therefore, literary canons can change with the shifting opinions and views of the people who influence them.

There are undoubtedly strong arguments for the use of a literary canon in settings and schools. The texts included are often good examples of literature, both the art of storytelling and of writing. They can provide rich and engrossing experiences beyond a child's own life and experiences. They enrich children's experiences of language and introduce wider creative use of language. Additionally, knowledge of texts that are regarded as 'good literature' inevitably brings elements of social and cultural capital. Therefore, the use of popular culture in schools and settings is not an either/or argument, (either a canon of literature or popular culture) but one that focuses on building provision from what is relevant, engaging and motivating, hence enabling children to learn. It is argued that popular culture uses what children know and enjoy as a starting point for their learning.

Why use popular culture in settings and schools?

There are a number of benefits to incorporating popular culture into provision in settings and schools.

- It enables learning to start from what children know and can do.

- It enthuses children and enhances their motivation to learn.

- It validates the experiences that children have outside school enabling them to feel that this knowledge is valued.

- It offers material that is familiar to children across different groups – often children from different cultural, racial, social and ability groups have shared interests and experiences within popular culture.

- It enables children to engage with different forms of meaning: linguistic, visual, audio, gestural, special and multimodal (all five together) (Cope and Kalantzis, 2000), which are a familiar part of their everyday worlds.

(Adapted from www.ite.org.uk/ite_topics/popular_culture_primary_english/002.html)

The benefits of incorporating popular culture in schools and settings is supported by the work of Lankshear (1997) and Luke (1993) who argue that only using a literary canon can work to benefit some children and disadvantage others. Dominant cultural understandings, they argue, are powerfully influenced and maintained by the dominant social class. These understandings then become the basis for a standardised curriculum in school and therefore norms against which all else is measured. Standardising provision in schools in this way means that anything that does not fit this standardised norm is made to appear substandard or lacking in some respect. Thus children who enter settings with the dominant social and cultural understandings find familiar provision which validates their experiences at home. In contrast, children who don't have this prior knowledge and understanding often find provision that does not reflect their experiences and this creates a divide between their interests and practices at home and those in the setting. Incorporating popular culture into what is done in schools and settings will, it is argued (Marsh, 2000), enable all children to learn through engagement with familiar content because it is content that starts from what children already know and can do.

Research evidence shows that where popular culture is incorporated into provision in settings and schools the benefits outlined above are clearly evident. See the theory focus below for an example of one such study.

THEORY FOCUS

Tubby custard (Marsh, 2000)

In her study Marsh and her colleagues introduced literacy activities related to Teletubbies in a nursery. The activities were designed to assess the potential that popular culture has for motivating children to sustain interest in language and literacy activities.

The study was conducted in two nurseries, both in inner-city areas. The nurseries served diverse communities including African-Caribbean, Pakistani, Bengali, Chinese, Yemeni, Somali and white British and Irish families. The majority of the children were *working class and, in many cases, lived in extremely difficult economic circumstances* (Marsh, 2000:122).

During the study a range of literacy-focused activities related to Teletubbies were introduced in the nursery including reading Tubby custard recipes, writing Tubby recipes for a range of food, reading Teletubby comics, making Teletubby comics, writing letters to the Teletubbies, writing Teletubby stories and designing advertisements to place in Teletubby comics. The activities were set up as part of the free-flow play activities so children were free to choose them.

The children's engagement with the literacy activity was marked: *The very moment that the Teletubbies were introduced a tremor of thrill ricocheted around the nurseries, which continued to reverberate throughout the sessions* (Marsh, 2000:124).

Outcomes included:

- a high level of interest in the activities – so much so that it was difficult to limit the group size;

continued

- excitement among the children;

- enthusiasm to write their own recipes in the writing area;

- motivation leading to the engagement of children who were normally disengaged with literacy-based activities – predominantly working-class boys;

- sustained interest in the literacy activities for significant periods of time – for example, reading the recipe and making and eating Tubby custard involved children for up to 30 to 35 minutes;

- persistence was a feature of children's involvement in the activities, both to become involved in the activity and to complete it;

- stimulation of oral work – there was lots of clearly enjoyable discussion around the programme and associated merchandise;

- pleasure in the activity and discussion which engendered a sense of community;

- links between different aspects of learning were made – for example, a link between the literacy skills in reading and writing recipes and scientific knowledge about the changing properties of materials.

Why do you think that this activity was so successful? Consider who benefited from this approach. How does this approach contribute to removing barriers to achievement for some children?

Investigate current popular culture for children. Who/what are the current people or artefacts that children are interested in? How could you use this in early years settings to support children's language and literacy learning?

ACTIVITY 2

It is important to be aware that as well as identifiable benefits there are concerns expressed about the use of popular culture in schools. These are issues that all practitioners need to have considered.

Consider these issues.

- *How may the use of a character or artefact act as an endorsement of a specific aspect of popular culture?*

- *What impact may this have on parents' choices?*

- *Should settings and schools engage in this type of relationship with commercial products?*

- *What do you think should be the criteria for using a particular character or artefact in a setting or school?*

- *What would you reject and why?*

continued

ACTIVITY *continued*

- *Which children would you use this approach with? Why?*

- *What are the disadvantages of placing too much emphasis on popular culture to the exclusion of other ideas and texts?*

SUMMARY

This chapter has discussed the importance of using what a child knows, can do and is interested in as the starting point for provision and interaction. Observation of children's play has been identified as the best way to establish children's current level of learning and their interests. Questions about who, what and how we observe children's play have been highlighted. The use of popular culture in settings, as an example of starting from the child, is outlined and case studies and research used to illustrate how this is manifest in practice. An activity provides the opportunity to reflect on some of the concerns expressed about the use of popular culture in settings and schools.

FURTHER READING

Fisher, J (1996) *Starting from the Child*. Buckingham: Open University Press.

Marsh, J and Hallet, E (2008) *Desirable Literacies: Approaches to Language and Literacy in the Early Years*, 2nd Edition. London: SAGE.

Marsh, J and Millard, E (2000) *Literacy and Popular Culture. Using Children's Culture in the Classroom*. London: SAGE.

Moyles, J (2010) *The Excellence of Play*, 3rd Edition. Berkshire: McGraw-Hill.

WEBSITES

www.UKLA.org

10 Rhymes, poems, songs, music and stories

This chapter enables you to understand:

- the importance of rhymes, songs and music;
- how rhymes, songs and music develop children's phonological awareness;
- why nursery rhymes are so important;
- the different ways in which young children engage with stories;
- the importance of stories, storying, storytelling and books;
- why babies need books;
- the value of using picture books with young children.

Introduction

Songs, poems, music and stories enrich all our lives. They have the potential to create joy, meaning and energy, feed our spirit and satisfy our human need for creativity. They are an integral part of adult lives in films, TV, books, playing and listening to live and recorded music, opera, musical theatre and dance. We use them as a significant part of national commemoration and celebration. We return to them in joy and in sadness because they connect with the deepest parts of who we are.

Songs, poems, music and stories often form part of what we *choose* to do. They are things that engage us and enrich our lives. This engagement means that we can often 'lose ourselves' in the activity, become engrossed in what we are doing and in doing so become less aware of the passage of time. This deep engagement with an activity is called flow.

Children who are introduced to rhymes, songs, music and stories in their earliest years can begin this creative journey and, in doing so, enhance their language acquisition and development and engage with the earliest stages of becoming literate.

THEORY FOCUS

Flow – Mihaly Czikszentmihalyi

In his book, *The Psychology of Optimal Experience* (2008), Czikszentmihalyi describes flow as:

> *being completely involved in an activity for its own sake. The ego falls away. Time flies. Every action, movement and thought follows inevitably from the previous one, like playing Jazz. Your whole being is involved, and you are using your skills to the utmost.*

Flow has its origins in the desire to understand the phenomena of how the people involved in something creative could persist single-mindedly, disregarding hunger, fatigue

continued

and discomfort, yet rapidly lose interest in the product once it had been completed. Flow research has its genesis in the desire to understand this phenomena of intrinsic motivation, in activity that is rewarding in and of itself quite apart from its end product and of any good that may come from completing the activity.

Being in 'flow' has the following characteristics:

- intense and focused concentration;

- merging of action and awareness;

- loss of awareness of self as a social actor;

- a sense that one can control one's actions in the sense that one can, in principle, deal with the situation because one knows how to respond whatever happens;

- distortion of temporal experience (typically a sense that time has passed faster then normal);

- experience of the action as intrinsically rewarding, such that often the end goal is just an excuse for the process.

The major contribution of flow activities and being 'in-flow' is to quality of life, bringing periods of deeply resonant optimal experience.

Why are rhymes, songs and music important?

First and foremost rhymes, poems, songs and music are important for children simply because they are fun, engaging, enriching and therefore worthwhile – we need no further justification than this. We can use them for the sheer joy in creativity and it is vital that we hold onto this in the current system which tends to value things predominantly for which curriculum skills and knowledge they develop.

Clearly, engagement with language in the form of song, rhyme and poetry extends and enhances the volume and quality of language that a child is exposed to. It offers the opportunity to use and enjoy language in different ways and in doing so provides another way of 'saying more than is necessary' (see Chapter 7), which in turn supports language acquisition and development.

These activities engage young children in a wide variety of language play. This playful (ludic) approach to language is important for our appreciation of language as a whole. Of course, we use language for communicating ideas and feelings but we also use it for fun (Crystal, 1998). We play around with, alter and manipulate language for playful effect. We use it to rhyme, pun and joke. We make up words and enjoy nonsense. We engage in language games. All of this requires a nuanced grasp of communication because language play often requires both linguistic and non-verbal signals to communicate meaning. Children engage in language play as well. Think about how often you hear children laugh at silly words or sentences they have made up; how they rhyme words for the sheer enjoyment of saying the rhyme; how they enjoy nonsense poems; how they will change words in songs to make them humorous; and how they will laugh at silly words and rhymes they put to familiar tunes. All this requires an increasingly sophisticated understanding and use of language which is embedded in rhymes, poetry and song.

Engagement with rhyme, poetry, song and music is also an important part of a child learning the prosodic structure of speech. In linguistics prosody refers to the use of pitch, loudness, tempo, rhythm and stress in speech to convey information about the structure and meaning of what we say. The prosodic structure of what we say enables us to use language in powerful and nuanced ways. Children need to learn this through interaction and engagement with language. Rhyme, poetry, song and music enable children to explore these aspects of interaction.

ACTIVITY *1*

When we speak our speech is organised into prosodic units, marked by intonation contours. This has a powerful effect on interaction.

Read the sentences below out loud. Change the meaning of the words each time by changing how you say the words. Communicate the meaning listed in the brackets.

- *What have you done? (sympathetic/angry/amazed)*

- *Come back. (demanding/begging/playful)*

- *Leave it alone. (coy/questioning/in danger)*

- *Why? (despairing/quizzical/cross)*

Notice how you can convey meaning using the same words but changing the prosodic structure. You have learned these ways of conveying meaning as you learned language. Young children need opportunities to learn and rehearse prosodic aspects of communication.

Rhymes, poems, songs and music are also one of the ways in which we develop aspects of phonological awareness. Indeed language play and a developing understanding of prosody are part of phonological development. Phonological development, in this context, is the ability to attend to and discriminate between sounds – not letter sounds (this is called phonemic or phonetic awareness and is part of phonology that comes later) but a broader range of sounds both within speech and the environment.

An important aspect of learning to talk is the development of the ability to break the sound stream into separate units and this requires that children can tune into sound. Children who hear and join in with rhymes, poems and songs and listen, make and move to music are able to begin the process of tuning into sound. They begin to be able to hear, discriminate and respond to what they hear, for example:

- hear the difference between percussive instruments when making music;

- hear and respond differently to vigorous and gentle music;

- hear rhyme and rhythm in clapping, skipping and action rhymes and games;

- hear and respond to a beat in music;

- maintain the beat and rhythm of the language in rhymes and poems;

- recognise and respond to real and nonsense words and alliterative and onomatopoeic words in rhymes and poems.

In these enjoyable ways children begin to tune into the sounds around them, including sound in language, and so enhance their language acquisition and development and begin the journey in literacy. As mentioned above, this is an important distinction. Engagement with rhymes, poems, songs and music has an intrinsic value and that is why children should be introduced to them. They have the capacity to create joy, meaning and energy, feed our spirit and satisfy our human need for creativity. It is alongside this that they offer an authentic and enjoyable way into learning, enhancing spoken language and becoming literate.

THEORY FOCUS

Steady beat competence

Steady beat competence refers to the child's ability to feel and express a steady beat. This timing is a fundamental skill. It is an important precursor to learning and development, including language acquisition, as it is thought to help us to detect patterns in incoming sensory information.

Weikart et al. (1987) found that in addition to sporting skill and musical performance, the ability to feel and express a steady beat is positively related to overall school achievement, including maths and reading achievement. Additionally, in another study Wright and Schweinhart (1994) found that many children entered pre-school unable to feel and express a steady beat.

Engagement in music activities and clapping, tapping and action games that focus on rhythm (and often rhyme) will support children in developing steady beat competence.

Nursery rhymes

There can be no discussion of the importance of rhyme and poetry in young children's lives without recognising the significance of nursery rhymes. A quick look at any bookshop or website for children's books will demonstrate how dominant nursery rhymes are. Strange perhaps as a closer look reveals that they relate a series of rather odd and often not very pleasant tales (Lockwood, 2011) – a farmer cutting the tales off blind mice, Humpty Dumpty not able to be mended after a fall, and a blackbird pecking off a maid's nose.

Yet these rhymes have enormous benefits in children's lives.

- They are fun – the oddball and slightly macabre often resonates with children.

- They provide a safe context in which to explore a wide range of emotions such as fear, excitement, anticipation, despair and joy.

- This entry to emotions is a powerful introduction to the world of poetry and books (Lockwood, 2011).

- They have strong cultural links (Brice Heath, 1983).

- They are part of the canon of literature.

- They engage children in word and language play.

- They encourage sensitivity to the sound of rhyme and rhythm and so support phonological development.

- Knowledge of nursery rhymes at three years old has been shown to link to later reading achievement (Bryant et al., 1995).

This engagement with rhyme, rhythm and wordplay supports and enhances language acquisition and development and, in addition, provides an introduction to the world of poetry. Indeed, it can be argued that this exploration of language *is* poetry (Whitehead, 2010).

THEORY FOCUS

The importance of nursery rhymes

This paper, outlined in the abstract below, provides evidence of the significance of knowledge of nursery rhymes to later reading attainment.

Abstract from: Bryant et al. (1989) Nursery rhymes, phonological skills and reading, p407.

Nursery rhymes are an almost universal part of young English-speaking children's lives. We have already established that there are strong links between children's early knowledge of nursery rhymes at 3:3 and their developing phonological skills over the next year and a quarter. Since such skills are known to be related to children's success in learning to read, this result suggests the hypothesis that acquaintance with nursery rhymes might also affect children's reading. We now report longitudinal data from a group of 64 children from the age of 3:4 to 6:3 which support this hypothesis. There is a strong relation between early knowledge of nursery rhymes and success in reading and spelling over the next three years even after differences in social background, I.Q. and the children's phonological skills at the start of the project are taken into account. This raises the question of how nursery rhymes have such an effect. Our answer is that knowledge of nursery rhymes enhances children's phonological sensitivity which in turn helps them to learn to read. This paper presents further analyses which support the idea of this path from nursery rhymes to reading. Nursery rhymes are related to the child's subsequent sensitivity to rhyme and phonemes. Moreover the connection between knowledge of nursery rhymes and reading and spelling ability disappears when controls are made for differences in these subsequent phonological skills.

Poetry

If we look at the world of poetry and when it works for us as readers and listeners, it will, to a great extent because it arouses feelings in us, gets us thinking, engages with ideas, gets us to look closely (or look afresh) at something, somebody or a relationship, offers us possibilities, takes us into a dream world … (Rosen 2011: 16)

Whitehead (2010: 24) describes play with the material of language as poetry. So, play with language, enjoyment of words, rhymes and rhythm, exploration and engagement with the range of emotions evoked through words is a young child's introduction to poetry. Perhaps poetry is associated in your mind with something overly intellectual or you recall finding poetry confusing at school. Try it again! Try something different – start with collections of poems so that someone has selected them for you to read; ask people what they have enjoyed; listen out for poems read at celebrations or commemorations; notice how films and TV programmes use them to evoke powerful emotions. As you begin to engage with poetry and share this with children, your enthusiasm will be communicated to them and, in turn, they will have access to all that poetry offers.

Lockwood (2011) in the book *Bringing Poetry Alive* explores the different ways in which poetry can, and should, be an integral part of young children's experience. However, careful consideration is required if we are to enthuse children about poetry. We need to be readers of poetry ourselves so that we can bring our experience and enthusiasm to activities and so that we are aware of the wealth of material available. We also need to consider how we use poetry in the setting. How do we introduce it? How do we maintain children's interest and engagement? How do we use it throughout our provision?

Choosing poems: Think carefully about what will engage children. What is fun? What is playful? What will elicit a rich emotional response? What has the potential for engaging the children?

Reading poems: Think about where and how you read poems to children. How can you create atmosphere? How can you invoke suspense or delight? How does the setting enhance the reading?

Performing poems: Think about how you could enhance the words in poems with your voice, actions, props or music. How could you involve the children in the performance? How could you bring the poem to life?

Responding to poems: What response can you expect from the children? How can you encourage them to listen carefully so that they are able to respond? If they are going to respond through language, what language do they need to enable them to respond? What other activities could you provide to facilitate children's responses, for example, drawing or painting, small world play or percussion instruments?

ACTIVITY 2

Choose a poem that you could use with children. Think carefully about your choice. It needs to have the potential to engage children. This could be done in a number of ways: invoke suspense or delight; be brought to life through performance or evocation of atmosphere; have the potential for responses through language, art, drama, small world play, music or role-play.

Find a poem that suggests this potential

For example,

- *In her poem* The Rings *Carol Anne Duffy evokes rings made of different materials alongside metaphoric understandings of the same material... 'with this silver ring I me wed to rivers, moonlight, midnight hours'. (Duffy, 2007)*

- *Grace Nichols (2000) in her poem* Cat-Shots *evokes photographs of a cat lying, sitting, standing, soaking, and behind the curtain.*

- *Michael Rosen (2006) in his poem* The Longest Journey in the World *relives a child's journey in darkness from the light switch to the bed 'so full of dangerous things – things that love dark places – things that breathe only when you breathe'.*

- *Quentin Blake's (1990) poems* All Join In *explore noise and silence, and include the wonderfully onomatopoeic 'Sorting Out the Kitchen Pans' 'DONG DANG BONG TING TANG BING BANG'.*

Think:

How would you engage children in the poem?

What would you:

- *say?*

- *do?*

- *use?*

How would you facilitate the children's response?

List the things that you think children would gain from engagement with your chosen poem.

Ways in which children engage with stories

Figure 10.1: Ways of engaging children with stories

The importance of books, stories and storytelling

Children engage with stories in many aspects of their lives – through the creation of narratives in their play, traditional routes such as books and TV programmes, drawing, and songs and music. Stories, in all their forms, are deeply embedded in what young children do, as is the authentic and enjoyable way in which they engage with language.

Books, stories and narrative in play are important for children. They engage with them at both a cognitive and affective level and they bring significant rewards.

- They are a rich source of enjoyment.

- Listening to (and eventually reading) and creating stories is, for many children, a flow activity.

- They offer an authentic way of extending and enhancing children's language capability.

- They are a source for the expression of a wide range of emotions.

- They provide an opening for sensitising children to the needs and feelings of others.

- They open up experiences beyond the child's own experience.

- They provide a safe way into understanding experiences beyond a child's own experience.

- They introduce children to voices other than their own, both in what they hear in stories and create in their play.

- They are a connection to children's own cultural heritage.

- They can connect children to a range of different cultural heritages; both in the content of the story and different cultural patterns of stories and storytelling.

- They enable children to see social patterns and relationships beyond their own experience.

- Children are able to explore social roles and perspectives through what they hear and what they create in their play.

- They encourage focused listening.

- Children who engage in 'storying' in their play and responses to books and storytelling absorb and explore notions of story structure, language and plot.

- They are an authentic introduction to literacy – both the forms and functions of reading and writing (see Part 3 of this book, *Becoming a reader and a writer*).

ACTIVITY 3

Choose a children's book to consider.

Read it through a few times, including out loud to yourself or others. As you read it, notice:

- *the language that is used;*

- *the voices that are used;*

- *the storyline;*

- *the emotional resonances in the story.*

Read back through the sections above on why books are important to children.

Now consider all that a child could learn from engagement with the text that you have chosen.

Reading to young children

Clearly, books are an important aspect of children's experience of stories and storytelling. Stories in books read to young children offer them the full range of experiences outlined above. Reading aloud to children also enables them to engage with the potential of reading. For very young children and beginning readers it acts as an apprenticeship to reading. Chambers (1991) describes reading to children as a 'loaning of consciousness' (Vygotsky, 1978) in that the parent or practitioner engages children in an activity that they are unable, at that moment, to undertake on their own. In doing so they entice children into the rich potential of stories in books (Goouch and Lambirth, 2011).

In terms of language acquisition and development hearing stories offers enriched language experiences. It introduces children to new and different ways of using language, including an enhanced vocabulary. Written language in texts is not just spoken language written down; it is a different way of using language and has a different function from the everyday. It includes different vocabulary, different patterns and rhythm of language use, rhyme, repetition and word play. Language in texts is considered and used carefully to convey meanings and create experiences. It goes beyond everyday language in that it aims to create experiences and provoke emotions through language (and image). Thus reading books to children enriches and enhances children's exposure to and therefore their experience of language.

Books and other reading matter need to be available across the pre-school setting so that they become part of the fabric of what children do. Practitioners not only need to provide the books but to actively engage children in using them, for example, providing and reading stories about princesses in a castle role-play area (choose carefully so as not to stereotype; use, for example, *The Twelve Dancing Princesses* (The Brothers Grimm); *The Paperbag Princess* (Munsch and Martchenko, 2009); *Princess Smartypants* (Cole 1996)); providing and reading stories about journeys on a bench near the bike shed; providing and reading stories about pets alongside a pet cage. Additionally, most pre-schools will have a story time or a group time when stories are read or told to the children. Storytime needs to be considered as carefully as any other activity.

The choice of book or story
- Is it matched to the children in the group?

- Does it have an engaging storyline?

- Look at the language potential. Does it enrich and enhance the children's experience of language, either through the language used, the text and/or the illustrations that support the text?

Preparation
- Read the book through, or learn the story well, if you are telling it, so that you know it well enough to tell it fluently and dramatically, and use any props effectively.

- Think about props that you could use to read, tell or retell the story engagingly, for example, puppets, a story chest, storyboard or music.

Reading the story
- Tell or read the story enthusiastically. Children will pick up on your enthusiasm.

- Enable the children to see the book pages as you read it.

- If you are reading a story, at points in the story reading trace your finger along the text. This alerts children to the difference between illustration and writing; it communicates one of the functions of writing (recording stories to be read) and it demonstrates left to right tracking in reading and writing.

- Read or tell the story all the way through to maintain the narrative and allow children to become engrossed in the story.

Following up the story telling
Talk about the story when you have read or told it all the way through. You could:

- look more closely at certain events or aspects of the story;

- talk about similar things that have happened to the children;

- continue parts of the story with 'What could happen next?' or 'What if?' questions;

- make up different endings;

- introduce rhymes or songs that link with the story;

- retell the story using props.

Using props to tell a story

A theatre group were going to visit the playgroup to do a performance of Goldilocks and the Three Bears. The theatre group wanted the children to be involved in the performance and so the practitioners thought that it was important that the children were familiar with the story before the theatre group's visit.

Initially, one of the practitioners read the story to the children. The following day she used a story chest to retell the story for the children. In it she had a wig, hats, bowls, spoons and a pillow. She used the props as she retold the story much to the children's delight. She then retold the story again encouraging the children to use the props when appropriate in the story.

The props were then put into the role-play area, which was set up as the three bears' house. Other opportunities were available in the setting for the children to engage with the story and characters, for example, in the dolls' house, in small world play (set up as a forest with a woodcutter's hut), making porridge, drawing the story on a long reel of paper mounted on the wall, acting out and recording on digital cameras in role-play.

When the theatre group came into the setting to do their performance the children were able to become fully involved in the experience as they were familiar with the story. This made the experience enjoyable and engaging, it formed positive associations with books, stories and theatre, and it contributed to the children's language and communication skills.

- *Why was it important that the children were familiar with the story before the theatre group came to the playgroup?*

- *Why do you think props were an effective way of retelling the story?*

- *Why did the staff use the props and provide other activities around the story?*

- *What would you do next to continue this enthusiasm that the children have for traditional tales?*

An enjoyable story time will undoubtedly develop and enhance a range of identifiable knowledge and skills. However, it is equally important that we see story time as just that – time to listen to a story with the aim of engaging children in an enjoyable and enriching experience. Goouch and Lambirth (2011) argue passionately for the importance of seeing books, stories and storying as valid in themselves and not just a means to an end to meet curriculum targets. They advocate seeing storytelling as an experience of what words can do in the form of rich narratives, exciting children about the potential of being a reader, and opening doors and enticing children into the exciting and emotional world of books and stories.

Babies need books

All the evidence suggests that children are born with the potential to acquire language and this potential develops after children are born through interaction with others. So babies have the capacity to learn language but they need to hear and use language to acquire and develop language. Reading books to babies provides one of the rich language experiences necessary for language acquisition and development, including an enjoyable and authentic engagement with rhyme and the rhythm of language.

Additionally, the close physical contact and individual attention that is involved in reading to babies builds positive associations for them towards books and stories. They offer opportunities for children to interact – verbally and non-verbally – in a calm and focused way. This positive orientation towards books as something enjoyable and worthwhile is immeasurably important as a child grows and learns.

The Bookstart project evaluation (Moore and Wade, 2003) outlined the importance of books for babies and demonstrated the impact that they had on children and families' engagement and interest in books and reading.

THEORY FOCUS

Bookstart

In recognition of the importance of books to babies and young children, the Bookstart project began in the early 1990s in Birmingham. Children received free books and advice on reading to babies and young children from health visitors.

Evaluation of the project compared children of two to three-years-old who received Bookstart packs with a sample of children who did not receive Bookstart packs. It showed that:

- 68 per cent of Bookstart children looked at books as one of their favourite activities (21 per cent for non-Bookstart);

- 75 per cent of Bookstart parents said they bought books as presents for their children (10 per cent for non-Bookstart);

Researchers observed parents sharing a book with their children, again comparing Bookstart families with a non-Bookstart sample.

- 83 per cent of Bookstart parents read the whole text compared with 34 per cent of non-Bookstart parents.

- 64 per cent talked about the story, compared with only 24 per cent.

continued

- 43 per cent encouraged the child to join in, compared with only 27 per cent.

- 68 per cent encouraged the child to make predictions, compared to 38 per cent.

Bookstart families shared more books but these findings also illustrate that the quality of the interaction between the parent and child was enhanced. Additionally:

- All the professionals involved in the project were overwhelmingly positive about the value of giving books to babies.

- Interviews with library staff demonstrated their firm commitment to the role that book sharing has to play in children's early development.

- The role of health visitors was crucial in introducing and explaining the pack – they saw an increase in parental interest in books and skill in sharing books with their children.

- Some parents that were harder to reach may need more support in using the gift of books effectively.

- Greater awareness of the needs of parents who have English as an additional language was needed.

Overall, bookstart was successful in generating positive attitudes to, and an interest in, books and book sharing in a wide range of families (Moore and Wade, 2003).

The initiative was extended to become a national programme which includes Bookstart packs of books given to young children: Bookstart baby pack; Bookstart+ for toddlers; Bookstart Treasure Chest 3–4s). There was an endorsement of the value of reading and rhyme through locally provided groups and sessions to promote books and reading and a continued commitment to supporting families in enjoying books with their children from as early an age as possible.

Using picture books with young children

It may seem strange that picture books can be supportive of language acquisition and development as they contain little or no written text. However, what they provide is a rich source for children's imagination and creativity. They have the potential to invoke pleasure, inspire fantasy, stimulate curiosity, develop empathy and personal understanding, and explore the art of story telling. At their most simple, picture books contain a narrative in pictures. This is easily accessible to very young children and provides a focus for interaction with others. Picture books can also contain highly sophisticated images that enable children to engage with them at different levels and in different ways. The Booktrust evokes an effective image of picture books as self-contained art galleries which children can visit over and over again, finding new ideas and resonances each time that they return to them.

Different types of picture books

The term 'picture books' can have various meanings.

In contrast to other books, in picture books the text and the pictures have, at least, equal importance.

- The narrative *is* the pictures – graphic books and wordless books. *The Boat (Mouse books)* by Monique Felix (2003). In this wordless book the little mouse scampers over the book and chews away the corner to reveal the ocean. He makes a paper boat as the ocean comes tumbling in and he sails away. The story is told in part through the mouse's beautifully expressive face.
  The Arrival by Shaun Tan (2007) is a wordless graphic novel that seems to tell the story of an immigrant arriving on Ellis Island. But this new country is like no place ever seen before. Giant crockery dominates the landscape, trollies fly, and people keep strange animal hybrids for pets. And yet the people in this alien landscape are familiar.

- The illustrations go beyond the text – *Hey, I love you!* by Whybrow and Reeve (2005) tells two stories in parallel; one is the text of a mouse following his mum from the safety of his den into the world because he forgot to tell her that he loves her, and another is told through the illustrations of a cat following the mouse who is following his mummy, close on his tail ready to pounce at any moment.

- The illustrations elucidate the text – *Monkey Puzzle* (Donaldson and Sheffler, 2000) tells the story of a monkey looking for his mummy. The butterfly who helps him offers lots of suggestions as to where he can find his mummy but to no avail because, as it turns out, baby monkeys look just like their mummies, unlike baby butterflies. The illustrations add an important visual elucidation of this confusion.

Ways of looking at picture books

Booktrust identifies five different ways of looking which are linked to the ways in which children, as they grow and learn, engage more fully with symbolic images. As children develop cognitively they increasingly begin to understand the meanings of images that are removed from real things. Thus children can begin to create meanings for images that are increasingly more fantastical, more witty, more rich with information and more para-doxical. However, these ways of looking are not hierarchical in the sense that they replace one another. Being able to see rich and complex meanings in images does not preclude the possibility of looking at pictures for pleasure. Older children (and adults) are able to see images in different ways and with different levels of understanding. Indeed, we may engage with a picture in all the different ways at the same time.

Way of looking at pictures	Stage of development
1. Looking for pleasure	Sensory and concrete learning
2. Inspiring fantasy	Imaginative and fantasy
3. Stimulating curiosity	Broadening horizons
4. Understanding others	Developing empathy and personal understanding
5. Exploring the making of art and stories	Higher cognitive thinking

Table 10.1: Ways of looking at pictures – demonstrating different stages of development

1. Initially, young children will look at images for pleasure – to seek out familiar things, to make links between objects, events and language, and to enjoy the sensory pleasure of engaging with images.

2. From the age of three, children begin to engage with, and enjoy, imagining characters, places, stories, people and events. Picture books have enormous potential to stimulate children's imagination and engage them in creative ideas and thinking.

3. Picture books can be likened to pictures in galleries and as such can stimulate curiosity. Pictures can act as a provocation to a range of questions. As children develop cognitively and begin to seek to understand and make meaning in their world, pictures can be part of children's fascination with who, what, why and how.

4. Empathy enables children to understand other people. Stories told in pictures and texts enable children to explore this emotional landscape in a safe way. Pictures have an immediacy that text lacks, and this enables us to tune into feelings and experiences. They encourage us to imagine 'what if?; to engage with feelings and situations beyond ourselves. As children grow and learn, picture books can support their developing awareness of self and others.

5. Older children are able to use their cognitive skills to analyse and interpret pictures both for their meaning and to understand how abstract ideas are embedded in narrative and illustration. They are able to understand how metaphorical images are used and created and how pictures can have multiple meanings. They are able to engage with abstract ideas and concepts embedded in images in picture books.

Adapted from Booktrust: www.booktrust.org.uk

Language is both used and enhanced through children's engagement with picture books. Language is the pre-eminent tool for thinking and communicating. In their engagement with picture books children will explore their ideas through language and communicate them through talk. There is also the potential to enhance children's language acquisition and development through interaction with them about the pictures and ideas in picture books. This is possible through engagement with picture books from the earliest stage of naming objects and people, through to articulation of the most complex abstract ideas embedded in the images.

Look at this image from Shaun Tan's (2001) book The Red Tree.

Figure 10.2: Image from The Red Tree

Read back through the different ways in which children can engage with images as they grow and learn.

- *How could you use this picture with children at each of the five stages of ways of looking?*

- *How would you use this picture to support children's talk and their language for thinking?*

SUMMARY

This chapter has outlined why rhymes, poems, songs, music and stories are important for children. It has emphasised that they have value in themselves as activities that enrich our lives. In addition to this, they support children's learning, including their language acquisition and development. The importance of nursery rhymes is recognised both for their benefits to language acquisition and as canonical texts. The chapter encourages you to consider poetry anew as something that, through language ... arouses feelings in us, gets us thinking, engages with ideas, gets us to look closely (or look afresh) at something (Rosen 2011:16) and asked you to consider how you could engage young children with poetry.

The different ways in which children engage with stories and storying are listed and the benefits outlined. Again, it is emphasised that stories have an intrinsic value and this should be considered to be as important as the knowledge and skills that stories and storying develop. The importance of reading out loud to children is outlined and suggestions

continued

SUMMARY *continued*

made for how to read or tell stories effectively. The reasons why babies need books is explored and research evidence of the effectiveness of this identified. Finally, the benefits of using picture books with children is outlined, including consideration of the different ways of looking at pictures and how language is used and enhanced in doing this.

FURTHER READING

Crystal, D (1998) *Language Play*. London: Penguin.

Czikszentmihalyi, M (2008) *The Psychology of Optimal Experience*. London: Harper.

Gamble, N and Yates, S (2008) *Exploring Children's Literature*, 2nd Edition. London: SAGE.

Goodwin, P (2008) *Understanding Children's Books*. London: SAGE.

Goouch, K and Lambirth, A (2011) *Teaching Early Reading and Phonics. Creative Approaches to Early Literacy*. London: SAGE.

Lockwood, M (2008) *Promoting Reading for Pleasure in the Primary School*. London: SAGE.

WEBSITES

www.readingforpleasure.org.uk

www.poetryarchive.org

www.booktrust.org.uk

www.literacytrust.org.uk

www.michaelrosen.co.uk

www.michaelmorpurgo.com

11 Creating a literate environment

This chapter enables you to understand:

- what is meant by a literate environment;
- why this is important in supporting children's language and literacy learning;
- how to create a literate environment.

Introduction

Evidence shows that children acquire and develop spoken language by being surrounded by talk, and that there is a powerful link between both the quantity and quality of the language that a child is exposed to and their acquisition and development of language skill (Hart and Risley, 1995: NLT, 2010; Sylva et al., 2003). One of the factors that has been identified as important in this development is that children hear and use talk in meaningful contexts: talking about daily events and interesting things that happen and recalling things that have happened (see Chapter 4). One of the reasons for this is that embedding interaction in a context enables children to use contextual information in support of their understanding.

Precisely the same can be said for reading and writing. Children do not wait until they go to school to engage with reading and writing. They are learning about reading and writing from a very young age as they observe other people reading and writing in their everyday lives. However, we are only able to learn what we experience (Purcell-Gates, 1995) so these understandings require that children grow and learn in a literate environment. When children grow up surrounded by everyday uses of reading and writing they begin to understand these literacy practices: it becomes part of the landscape of their lives. This understanding of the purposes of literacy is the beginning of learning to read and write.

What is meant by a literate environment?

A literate environment is one in which there are high levels of talk (where people say more than is necessary: see Chapter 4) and where reading and writing are everyday, purposeful activities.

At home a literate environment includes:

- *talk as social interaction* that goes beyond functional uses of language and engages in discussion, explanation, questioning, pondering and language play (see Chapter 4);

- *reading and writing in support of household jobs and routines*: lists, forms, emails, notes, reading labels and instructions; shopping online;

- *reading and writing to communicate*: texting, emails, cards, letters, social network sites;

- *reading and writing for pleasure*: books, magazines, newspapers, internet, social network sites;

- *reading and writing associated with work done at home*; reading books, reports or plans, writing reports or preparing invoices, sending and receiving emails.

CASE STUDY

A literate environment at home

Hannah and her mum were going shopping. They planned to do a few jobs first, including some food shopping, and then meet Hannah's friend Phoebe and her mum in a café. Before they left home, Hannah sat with her mum as she wrote a list of the food that they needed to buy. They also signed and addressed a birthday card to Hannah's granny. Before they left the house Hannah's mum texted her friend to let her know what time they would be in town.

On the way to town they posted the card and Hannah's mum explained that the address on the front showed where Granny lives so that the post office knew where to take the card.

In the shops Hannah watched intently as her mum read the information alongside the products about prices and offers before choosing which item Hannah was to put in the basket. Before they went to pay, her mum read out the list and they made sure that they had remembered everything.

As they left the shop, Hannah's mum texted her friend to say that they were on their way to the café. When they arrived, Phoebe was sitting with her mum and they were looking at the menu deciding what to have to drink. Hannah and her mum joined them and Hannah's mum read the list of drinks available so Hannah could choose. Phoebe's mum went to buy the drinks and Hannah and her mum started to tell Phoebe what they had been doing all morning.

- *List the different ways that Hannah engaged with reading and writing.*

- *What makes these experiences meaningful?*

- *What do you think she learns from this?*

- *What other ways may Hannah have engaged with reading and writing in her morning out with her mum?*

In settings a literate environment includes:

- *talk* that goes beyond organisational talk and brief social interactions and actively engages children in talking through commentary, discussion, questioning, pondering, explanation and language play (see Chapter 7);

- *use of reading and writing in routines*: registration, name places, lists, naming paintings, labels on toy storage for 'packing-away-time', letters home;

- *reading and writing for pleasure*: stories, poems, rhymes and songs;

- *reading and writing around the setting*: peg labels, display labels, directions, instructions, labels on toy storage;

- *observing and using emergent reading and writing during focused activities*: practitioner writes the children's descriptions of their models and reads them out at group time to the other children before putting them on display; practitioner reads out instructions on the back of packets of seeds to explain how to plant them; practitioner Googles, reads out and refers to a recipe on a website as part of a baking activity;

- *provision of resources so children can engage in emergent reading and writing during activities*; books, pencils and paper, computers.

The effect of providing a literate environment both at home and in schools and settings is that children gradually come to know the ways in which talk, reading and writing are used and begin to internalise that that they are useful and meaningful skills to have.

CASE STUDY

Playing police

The boys in the nursery loved playing at police. They created and played out elaborate narratives about goodies and baddies. All the narratives ended with the police chasing the baddies, arresting them, taking them down to the police station and locking them up.

The staff had provided dressing-up clothes and equipment and, with the children's help, converted an area of the nursery into a police station and cells. This included opportunities for reading and writing through the provision of labels, signs, directions, name badges, posters, paper and pens, and a computer. Most of the boys were able to write emergently using marks on the page and to use contextual clues to work out what the signs, posters, directions and labels were saying.

The boys enjoyed playing police over a number of days and the staff enhanced their play through joining in and introducing different ideas into the play. On one day the staff joined in and introduced some specific vocabulary, such as suspect, charge, interview and crime scene. On another day they joined in and introduced the idea of using digital cameras and the computer to take pictures of the crime scene and the suspects and label them. On another day they introduced the idea of using police notebooks to record what had happened at the scene of the crime, and what the suspects said when they were interviewed at the police station.

Engagement with talk, reading and writing in these ways gradually and meaningfully introduced reading and writing to the boys as necessary, useful and important skills to have and be able to use.

continued

CASE STUDY *continued*

- List the ways in which the children were encouraged to engage in talk and literacy practices in their play.

- What do you think the children learned from this engagement with talking, reading and writing?

- Why did the staff introduce aspects of reading and writing into the play?

- What other literacy practices could you introduce into police play?

Why is this important?

When children are involved in purposeful literacy practices they learn both the functions and the forms of reading and writing in an authentic and meaningful way. They come to know what it means to read and write. This knowledge and understanding provides both a context and incentive to engage with learning to read and write as children move into school and are introduced to the more formal aspects of literacy.

DEFINITION

Functions: what we use reading and writing for.

Forms: how we read and write.

Understanding the functions and forms of literacy is important conceptual knowledge as children learn to read and write. Understanding the functions of literacy means that children begin to understand why reading and writing are important and necessary skills to have. For example, children learn that we use reading and writing for:

- enjoyment and creativity;

- finding information;

- conveying information;

- organising information;

- recording information;

- directions;

- instructions.

Understanding that this is what reading and writing enables us to do means that learning to read and write becomes meaningful – we need to read and write to enable us to do these things.

It is similar with the forms of language. The more children are exposed to reading and writing in real and meaningful contexts, the greater their understanding is likely to be of necessary concepts in beginning reading and writing, such as:

- the relationship between speech and print: writing is the setting down, or recording, of speech (as 'squiggles-on-a-page'); there are differences between written language and spoken language – it is related but different; reading is decoding writing ('squiggles on a page') into speech;

- we track left to right when we read and write;

- we predominantly track top to bottom on pages when we read and write (this is not always the case when reading from websites and in some children's books which use words and text creatively);

- print-related terms, such as 'letter' and 'word'.

As children interact with print they begin to sort out and acquire these concepts. They begin, as Purcell-Gates (1995:64) says, to *travel the route of children who progress from noticing the 'stop' sign and its role in directing drivers to stop, to understanding that the letters s-t-o-p say 'stop'.*

CASE STUDY

Birds and bugs

The Reception class children had become fascinated by the bird and bug boxes in the garden. They regularly spent time watching the birds as they went in and out of the bird boxes and used the bug boxes to look at the bugs in the garden. The staff joined them in looking at the birds and bugs through magnifiers and binoculars. The children were full of questions about which birds and bugs they were observing and what they ate and where they lived.

Alongside the children, staff looked up this information in books and on the internet. They printed out sheets of information and pictures of birds and bugs, which they laminated and put up as posters in the garden, along with books, for children to refer to.

The staff also provided digital cameras for the children to take photographs of the birds and bugs and created a wildlife gallery of what is in the garden. The children decided on the labels and captions and the staff wrote these out alongside the children, modelling writing. The staff also read the information to the children and they annotated it with drawings to show what the birds and bugs ate and where they lived.

- *What opportunities are there in this activity for children to learn about the functions of reading and writing?*

- *What may they have learned?*

- *What opportunities are there in this activity for children to learn about the forms of reading and writing?*

- *What may they have learned?*

- *How do these opportunities contribute to children becoming literate?*

When children have little or no early engagement with high levels of talk and literacy practices, evidence suggests that their move into literacy becomes more difficult (Purcell-Gates, 1995). We are only able to learn what we experience (Purcell-Gates, 1995), therefore, not only do these children have limited speech and language, which in turn affects learning (Hart and Risley, 1995: NLT, 2010; Sylva et al., 2003), but they often lack the conceptual understandings that facilitate literacy learning. This means that these children start school and move straight into the formal aspects of literacy learning (phonics, grapheme-phoneme correspondence, segmenting and blending) without the necessary contextual understanding to make this learning purposeful and meaningful. At worst, literacy for these children often becomes just something that they do at school, something that is often quite challenging and that has very little meaning or purpose beyond school.

THEORY FOCUS

A world without print

Victoria Purcell-Gates (1995) sought to understand what it is, cognitively and linguistically, that young children learn about print before formal schooling and the ways in which this affects their success when beginning formal instruction in reading and writing at school.

Her work was conducted in America. She worked with a family – a mother and child, Jenny and Donny – who couldn't read or write anything beyond their names. This family presented 'a rare opportunity – in a society such as ours where print is so pervasive – to explore the role that experiences with print do and do not play in young children's development as literate beings' (Purcell-Gates, 1995:41).

Donny's world was virtually void of functional literacy events beyond the signing of names and minimal marks on a calendar to indicate appointments. Other than this no one in his immediate family or home used print for any other purpose. Outside the home, Jenny (Donny's mum) used physical markers to find shops, offices and products. She used the size and design of buildings, signs, logos and pictures. When she was unable to work things out, she would speak to friends, for example, instructions for cooking on packets. Family activities similarly did not involve reading or writing in any form – they hunted, fished, cooked, gardened, sewed and visited friends and family.

Interestingly, there was printed material in the home: a bible, some cross-stitch designs of religious verses, a calendar and some boxes of books in the loft. These were taken down occasionally and 'read' to the boys by looking at the pictures and making up a story. However, these literacy objects played little or no role in the daily life of the family.

Donny was essentially growing up in a world without print. Although he lived in a place and a country surrounded by print he did not experience it. He didn't notice it or understand its uses.

In his pre-school years Donny learned very little in terms of the concepts associated with emergent literacy. This meant that he was coming to formal school learning without some of the fundamental concepts underpinning learning to read and write. After two years in school he:

continued

- *understood that print could encode names; he could write his name and read it when it was pointed out;*

- *knew that a book was for reading, but 'reading' often meant making up a story according to the pictures – just like at home – the black squiggles that we know to be print were often an irrelevance for Donny;*

- *knew letters were named and printed as isolated units of the alphabet – by the end of his second year in school he could accurately recognise two-thirds of letters and write about 90 per cent of them;*

- *could 'do school' – fill in worksheets that involved circling words and follow books when people read, although this was often not matched to what the teacher was doing.*

Purcell-Gates (1995) concluded that children will learn about the forms of print according to the functions that they see for print in their lives. Therefore, because Donny grew up in a home without print and had no conceptual understanding of the functional uses of print in his life, school-based teaching, focused on the forms and symbolic nature of print, had little meaning or relevance to Donny. He acquired some knowledge and skill and was able to perform certain school-based literacy tasks but they lacked meaning or purpose because they lacked an underpinning conceptual framework and relevance to his life beyond school.

How to create a literate environment

A literate environment requires that children are surrounded by talk, reading and writing, that it is embedded in everyday activities and interactions and that it is part of the landscape of children's lives at home and in settings and schools.

One of the important aspects of this is practitioners' attitudes towards literacy, particularly reading and books. The evidence shows that when practitioners are interested and engaged by books and reading this is evident in their provision and interaction and so they pass this enthusiasm onto the children. What we do is vitally important in influencing children's orientation towards, books, reading and writing (Cremin et al., 2008; Sylva et al., 2003).

Teachers as Readers: Building Communities of Readers (Cremin et al., 2008)

The purpose of this study was to improve teacher's knowledge and use of literature in order to help them increase children's motivation and enthusiasm for reading, especially for children who are less successful in literacy.

continued

One of the main aims of the project was to *develop reading teachers who read*. The project showed that teachers' enriched knowledge of children's literature and other texts transformed their conceptions of reading. This resulted in marked improvements in reading environments in the classroom, reading aloud, talking about books, recommending books and time for independent reading.

This positive orientation supported children's reading for pleasure, which has been shown to positively impact on children's attainment, achievement, disposition and desire to read (Cremin, Bearne, Goodwin, and Mottram, 2008).

One of the study's conclusions was that *reading teachers act as actively engaged role models for children's reading.*

In settings practitioners need to ensure that children are surrounded by, and involved in, creating a literate environment by, for example:

- actively engaging in talking with the children – saying more than is necessary (see Chapters 4 and 7);

- labelling toy boxes and cupboards – with both pictures and words;

- putting up signs – 'toilet', 'kitchen', 'cloakroom' etc.;

- labelling displays – this can be done alongside the children who can be involved in deciding what the captions should say and observe them being written, typed and printed;

- labelling role-play areas with appropriate signs, captions and charts;

- providing opportunities to engage with authentic literacy in play (see below), for example, providing menus, price lists, appointment books, maps, instructions, leaflets, notebooks and pencils, reference books, charts etc.;

- reading and enjoying books, both with the children and independently;

- ensuring that books are included as part of the resources in activities;

- using the computer as an integral part of activities, for example, to access information, word process, play games and activities;

- completing routine tasks alongside the children, for example, doing the register, naming and handing out letters, completing lists;

- making good use of opportunities for literacy in activities (see case study below);

- labelling children's work as they observe you and explaining why you are doing this;

- drawing children's attention to reading and writing in the setting, both to enable them to notice it in their environment and see when and how you engage in reading and writing.

High standards

All lettering and writing in a setting must be of a high standard as it is providing a model of writing for the children. For example, it should show:

- proper use of upper and lower case lettering;
- correct spelling;
- correct punctuation;
- letters formed correctly;
- writting from left to right in a straight line.

When labelling in languages other than English some other rules may apply. It is, of course, essential that labelling in other languages is also written correctly. Parents and local community members are valuable sources of information for this.

CASE STUDY

Making good use of opportunities for literacy in activities

Following a visit to the nursery by one of the parents with her baby the staff noticed that the children had begun to play at mummies and babies. They decided to use this interest when changing the role-play area.

- *Initially they read a book to all the children about a baby going to a baby clinic.*

- *Following this they had a discussion with the children about setting up the baby clinic in the nursery and what they would need and use.*

- *The next day the book was put out with a large sheet of paper and the children were encouraged to come and record, alongside a member of staff, what they thought was needed. Some of them used the book as a guide or reminder, looking at the pictures and asking the member of staff to read passages to them. Some children recorded their ideas in pictures and symbols while some used emergent writing with appropriate initial letters and/or phonetically plausible attempts at words.*

- *Additionally, staff put information about baby products on the computer for children to find, look at, record, download or print.*

- *The teacher put the items into a list and at group time the children and teacher read the list together to decide which of these resources they had in the nursery and which they would need to acquire. One of the children highlighted the list to show what they could find and what was needed.*

- *The following day small groups of children were given a list of things to collect and tick off as they found them.*

- *Once everything had been gathered together they returned to the main list and checked it was all there before taking it to the role-play area.*

- *The staff engaged children in devising and producing captions, signs, directions and labels for the clinic.*

ACTIVITY 1

Read through the case study above and make sure that you understand how the teachers made good use of opportunities for literacy when setting up the baby clinic. Identify when the children were engaged in reading and writing.

Plan how the staff would engage children in devising and producing captions, signs, directions and labels for the clinic. Highlight where in the plan you have provided opportunities for literacy.

SUMMARY

This chapter has explained what is meant by a literate environment. It has identified the benefits of growing and learning in a literate environment as gradually coming to know the ways in which talk, reading and writing are used, and beginning to internalise that that they are useful and meaningful skills to have. It is acknowledged that these are important concepts for children to have as they learn to read and write. Ways of creating a literate environment in a setting are outlined and you were asked to extend a case study to demonstrate your understanding of this. There are a number of case studies throughout the chapter that illustrate what is meant by a literate environment at home, in schools and in settings. The research that underpins this practice is cited.

FURTHER READING

Brock, A and Rankin, C (2008) *Communication, Language and Literacy from Birth to Five.* London: SAGE.

Goouch, K and Lambirth, A (2011) *Teaching Early Reading and Phonics. Creative Approaches to Early Literacy.* London: SAGE.

Hall, N (1997) *The Emergence of Literacy.* Sevenoaks: Hodder and Stoughton.

Marsh, J and Hallet, E (2008) *Desirable Literacies: Approaches to Language and Literacy in the Early Years,* 2nd Edition. London: SAGE.

Morrow, LM (1990) Preparing the classroom environment to promote literacy during play. *Early Childhood Research Quarterly,* 5: 537–554.

Teale, W and Sulzby, E (1986) *Emergent Literacy Reading and Writing.* Norwood, New Jersey: Ablex Publishing Corporation.

Whitehead M (2010) *Language and Literacy in the Early Years 0–7,* 4th Edition. London: SAGE.

WEBSITES

www.literacytrust.org.uk

Part 3
Becoming a reader and a writer

12 Understanding literacy

This chapter enables you to understand:

- what is meant by literacy;
- how young children become literate.

Introduction

Being literate is a vital skill. We live in a literate world that places high value on reading and writing and so we all need to learn to read and write. As early years practitioners it is important that we think carefully about how we support children to become literate. Both reading and writing are foremost a way of communicating (Whitehead, 2010), and this needs to be emphasised in the early years. Naturally, children will need to learn the forms that are used to communicate through reading and writing (phonics, pencil grip, letter formation) but, for young children, these need to be a function of the communicative process and not learned as decontextualised skills.

It is in the early years that children become literate because in these years children move into literacy. At home and in settings children develop the initial interest, knowledge and skill to enable them to become a reader and a writer. Talking, reading and writing are learned skills. Children learn through interaction with others in their environment, and becoming literate requires that young children have experiences that value literacy, and that they are able to engage in activities that use literacy in authentic ways.

What is literacy?

Speech uses words, sentences and prosody to communicate with others. Writing represents this spoken language symbolically and reading is the process of understanding and creating meaning from this representation.

Historically, writing and reading have had profound effect on the development of people and societies. Until there was mass education in Western Europe in the nineteenth century most people could not read and write. Reading and writing were restricted to a powerful elite who were able to use it in ways that suited their purposes. Nowadays, in western Europe, the vast majority of people are able to read and to write, and it is regarded as a fundamental aspect of being able to function well and make a contribution to society. Indeed, Article 28 of the United Nations Convention on the Rights of the Child recognises children's right to an education, including the opportunity to become literate. Being literate enables us to participate fully in society. It means that we are able to function well within a society that assumes a competence in reading and writing; it enables us to become educated and to work which, in turn, offers us economic stability;

it enables access to information, through the internet, books, magazines and newspapers and this, should we choose it, gives us a voice in society. Being literate also offers a source of delight and enjoyment through books and literature.

How do children become literate?

Literacy used to be considered something that happened in school; it was seen as an individual, linear activity. There used to be little acknowledgement of the learning that took place prior to children starting statutory schooling and formal literacy teaching. This view has changed. It is now accepted and understood that early literacy is learned, rehearsed and understood through activities and experiences that take place at home, in communities and in pre-school settings before children start school, as well as in school. This period of early literacy is necessary to the acquisition of conventional literacy. It is the period in which children are learning and developing the necessary interest, knowledge and skill to enable them to communicate in different ways for different purposes. This requires them to:

- become aware and interested in reading and writing (How do we use reading and writing? Why are they important and useful? What purpose do they serve?);

- learn to symbolise;

- have opportunities to represent their thoughts, ideas and experiences in a range of ways such as drawing, building, mark-making, use of ICT, and combinations of these modes of representation;

- begin to engage with the forms of representation that mark the beginnings of conventional writing and reading.

Understanding the purposes of reading and writing

Through their exposure to reading and writing in real and meaningful situations children begin to understand the reasons why we need to read and write. They begin to internalise the notion that reading and writing are valuable skills to have. When children have experiences of seeing and being involved in literate activities that serve a function in people's lives, including being a source of pleasure and delight, they effortlessly absorb the significance of reading and writing. It becomes understood as a purposeful and meaningful part of life and this has a profound effect on children's engagement with writing and reading.

THEORY FOCUS

Growing up in a literate environment

Denny Taylor studied children from highly literate families. Her account of this research illustrated the experience of children who were growing up in families where literacy is part of the very fabric of life. Reading and writing were woven into virtually every aspect of the families' activity. Literacy gave them both status and identity within their community.

continued

The children in Taylor's study were read to from birth. They were exposed to notes written by parents to siblings and by siblings to parents. They participated in games that involved printed directions and created play that required the printing of such items as labels for a lemonade stand or a list of rules for a newly formed club. They observed their parents reading books, newspapers, notes from school and letters from relatives and others, and they were exposed daily to shop signs and advertisements in the environment and on the television. It is within this literate context that these children learned much about the nature and forms of written language.

Cited in Purcell-Gates (1995: 48)

Representation and symbolising

The ability to represent the world symbolically is an essential part of learning to read and write. This understanding and skill develops as part of children's wider cognitive abilities.

- Initially, children come to know and understand through being active – they engage with the world through their senses and internalise these actions and images. This is described by Piaget as the sensorimotor stage of development. Children's understandings tend to be immediate and concrete.

- In gesture, through the acquisition and development of language and through role-play, children begin to use symbols: that is, use one thing to represent another. For example, a wave of the hand to mean bye-bye; a word (horse) to represent a concrete object (a horse); a doll to represent a baby. This is evidence of a child's early ability to symbolise.

- As children grow, develop and broaden their experiences this symbolising begins to appear in the form of drawing, modelling and mark-making and in a child's ability to engage with symbols as 'reading'. This is evidence of a child's growing ability to understand and represent ideas, thoughts, imaginings and experiences in symbolic ways.

Look at your hand. Touch and feel it. What you see and experience is the concrete object. This is sensorimotor experience – it is an action experienced through your senses of touch and sight. It is real!

We can also represent a hand symbolically. It is not real but we use the symbols to represent the object, and because we can 'read' the symbol we understand what it is representing.

We can represent a hand as shown in Figure 12.1.

continued

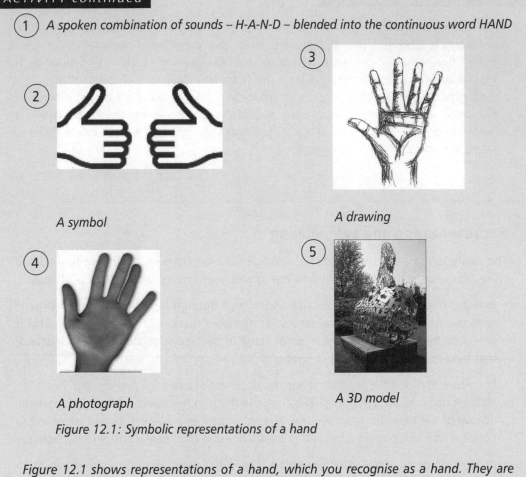

ACTIVITY *continued*

① *A spoken combination of sounds – H-A-N-D – blended into the continuous word HAND*

②

A symbol

③

A drawing

④

A photograph

⑤

A 3D model

Figure 12.1: Symbolic representations of a hand

Figure 12.1 shows representations of a hand, which you recognise as a hand. They are meaningful symbols that stand in place of the real thing. This ability to symbolise, to use one thing to represent another, is a vital part of early literacy as it is a skill required in reading and writing. Letters, written in combination, are symbols for words. Reading and writing is the ability to understand and use these symbolic representations of words.

Using symbols to create meaning

In learning to read and write, children come as thoroughly experienced makers of meaning (Kress, 1997: 8).

Long before children come to writing they use a range of symbolic ways to represent what they know and can do, and what they are thinking. From continued experience children's earliest use of symbols to communicate meaning (a thumb-up for good, a box for a helmet) change and develop. They begin to communicate meanings in a wider variety of ways using toys, materials and equipment (they build, they draw, they model, they engage in craft activities and role-play). In these ways children come to understand, make and represent meaning, and communicate ideas, thoughts, imaginings and experiences in symbolic ways.

Kress (1997) argues that children have this greater scope to create meaning in different modes because they are not restricted by adult conceptualisations about what are appropriate or correct ways. They are not constrained by having to represent ideas, thoughts and experiences through language: spoken, written or read. Children focus on what best fits the purpose; what is available for use. This results in different ways of meaning-making using different modes.

CASE STUDY

Young children making meaning and representing thought

Sara, aged three years and ten months, had seen a hedgehog in her garden on the way into nursery. Her dad told the staff about it as he dropped her off. The practitioner asked Sara about the hedgehog but she was reluctant to say anything. Later on in the session however, the practitioner noticed that in a number of ways Sara was exploring the experience of seeing the hedgehog and using the different materials and equipment available to communicate this experience.

First, she went over to the craft table and drew two slightly distorted semicircular shapes. She used the fat crayons to draw short spiky marks on each shape. On one she used blue, pink, yellow, green and orange and on the other a light orangey-brown. The many-coloured hedgehog was done in larger, bolder more energetic strokes than the other one. The practitioner overheard Sara telling her friend that one was a good hedgehog and one was a bad hedgehog.

Later in the morning Sara and a friend went over to the dressing-up area and emptied all the clothes out of the basket onto the floor. They then carefully put some of them back into the bottom of the basket to create a nest. Sara then curled up inside the basket and warned her friend, 'Don't stroke me because I am prickly'.

Towards the end of the morning Sara had made a clay hedgehog. It was a clay ball with matchsticks stuck into it. She brought it with her to listen to the story.

Adapted from an idea in Kress (1997)

- *List the ways in which Sara communicated and represented her thoughts about what she had seen.*

- *In what ways is this different to how adults would communicate their experience?*

- *Why is this different?*

- *Read the description of her drawings carefully. What do you think that she was trying to communicate in her drawings?*

- *What else can you learn from the representations of her experience?*

- *What does this tell you about Sara's understanding of representing things symbolically?*

- *Why is this important as she learns to read and write?*

Moving into using conventional writing and reading

As children grow and learn they continue to use a range of ways to communicate meaning and understanding (drawing, modelling, craft activities, role-play) and letters and numbers begin to appear as part of this. This is evidence of their increasing awareness of print and its uses, for example, they may begin to put approximations of letters in their drawing as a label for what they have drawn. This will often be purposeful and have meaning for the child as they will tell you what it says. This also demonstrates that children have a concept of reading – that reading involves making meaning from letters on the page. Interestingly, some children very quickly realise that the meaning of the 'word' is always the same, that is, what is written stays the same each time that it is read. Other children take longer to understand this and will change the meaning of what they have written each time you ask them what it says. These are important conceptual leaps for children. This use of letters and numbers to symbolise meaning marks the beginning of children acquiring conventional literacy.

This opportunity to explore meaning-making in different and developmentally appropriate ways is significant for the ease with which children come to reading and writing (and recording number). If children have had these opportunities, including the time to explore symbolic meaning-making in substantial and sustained ways, the move into conventional literacy tends to be significantly easier. It means that learning to read and write are small steps from firm foundations.

It is important to be aware that these are not hierarchical developmental stages. There is an observable pattern and progression but children will continue to use different modes to represent their understanding throughout childhood, including once they have learned to read and write with reasonable proficiency. This would accord with the view of Kress (1997) that children, in contrast to adults, tend to use the measure of 'aptness for' rather then convention, when representing their ideas.

ACTIVITY 2

The relationship between early literacy and conventional literacy

Imagine an iceberg. Only the tip of the iceberg is visible; most of it is under the sea. The part of the iceberg that is under the sea is unseen but it is immense in size, and in proportion to the tip. The tip of the iceberg that can be seen cannot exist without what lies underneath the water, huge, unseen, but vital in building and supporting the iceberg tip.

This is a wonderful metaphor for literacy. Reading and writing are the tip of the iceberg. They are obvious skills that can be seen and used. Early literacy provides the relatively unseen, but necessary, building blocks and support for the observable skills of reading and writing. Successful acquisition of reading and writing depend on early literacy practices.

- *Create your own metaphor for the relationship between early literacy and conventional literacy. Remember: conventional literacy is obvious and observable. Early literacy is less obvious but necessary to the conventional literacy. Conventional literacy depends upon early literacy.*

Roots of literacy

'Roots of literacy' is a metaphor used by Yetta Goodman (1986). Goodman suggests that as we observe children we can see them inventing, discovering and developing under-standings about literacy as they grow up in a literate environment. Her work on early literacy also concludes that children are alive to literacy and developing skills and concepts long before they become conventionally literate.

Goodman argues that the beginnings of literacy occur as children become aware and begin to realise written language makes sense and, simultaneously, begin to wonder *how* it makes sense. It is in this exploration of the literate environment that children develop the 'roots of literacy'. These roots include:

- print awareness in situational contexts: children become aware that print carries mean-ing as they see it used in day-to-day situations such as on packaging, signs and logos;

- print awareness in connected discourse: children become aware of the print in written material such as books, magazines, newspapers, letters;

- functions and forms of writing: children become aware of the many ways in which we use print in our day-to-day lives, they begin to notice how we write and read, and that reading and writing are different;

- oral language about written language: children begin to talk about reading and writing, which reflects their growing awareness of the uses of reading and writing in a literate society, and they begin to learn words that refer to language, such as letter or word;

- metalinguistic and metacognitive awareness about written language: children develop the conceptual ability and the language to enable them to talk about language – this means that they are able to conceive of language as something that can be talked about, both in terms of its constituent parts (a word, a letter) and about how and why it is used.

Goodman continues her metaphor of 'roots' in her observation that children need the fer-tile soil of a literate environment (see Chapter 10) in which to grow and learn. In this way, early literacy will emerge as children seek out and explore literacy practices. The knowl-edge and skill that arises from this engagement is often referred to as emergent reading and writing.

Metalinguistic awareness

Metalinguistic awareness is the ability to reflect on language as an object (Sulzby and Teale, 1991). This ability is an essential part of the transition into conventional literacy. When children are able to see and reflect on language it enables them to identify and talk about the constituent parts of language, for example, a letter, a word, or about lan-guage itself, asking questions such as does it make sense and how can we make it so? They develop a language for talking about language and in doing so their tacit knowledge becomes explicit.

Take the example of 'a word'. Long before children understand what 'a word' is they can use words effectively. However, their knowledge about what a word is is tacit – it remains known but unspoken. To enable them to learn to read and write, a child's understanding of 'a word' needs to be made explicit – known and expressed. They need the conceptual understanding and the language to be able to talk about language – this is called metalinguistic awareness.

Consider that as children are introduced to conventional literacy teachers use phrases such as:

- 'What does this word begin with?'

- 'Which word begins with an 's'?'

Clearly, children who understand the concept of 'a word', and are able to talk about it, are at an advantage in these situations when learning to read and write.

The role of the adult is vital in the process of children acquiring metalinguistic awareness. It is acquired through interaction that facilitates both language use and reflection on language that draws this knowledge into consciousness (Gombert, 1992). For some children this process is embedded in how they learn to talk. Within some families language is treated both as a form of communication and as something to be discussed and enjoyed and analysed, so this orientation to language is transmitted as children grow and learn (Olsen, 1988). Other children will need to develop this knowledge and understanding in schools and settings, so in their interaction practitioners need to alert children to the language that they are using and enable them to notice and talk about language.

CASE STUDY

Noticing words

It was story time. Imogen decided to do some nursery rhymes stories with the children but to change things around. She settled the children down and asked them to listen very carefully.

> *'Hickory Dickory Dock.*
> *Jamie ran up the clock*
> *The clock struck one*
> *The mouse ran down*
> *Hickory Dickory Dock.'*

The children laughed out loud.

She asked them what she had done and they pointed out that she had said 'Jamie' instead of 'mouse'.

Imogen reflected back what they had said but rephrased it,

'Yes, I replaced the word 'mouse' with the word 'Jamie'.

They all then said the rhyme through a few times, putting different children's names in place of 'mouse'.

Then Imogen asked then to close their eyes, listen very carefully, and spot the word that she was changing this time.

---

continued

CASE STUDY *continued*

'Hickory Dickory Dock,
The mouse ran up the clock,
The clock struck three,
The mouse ran down,
Hickory Dickory Dock.'

Very quickly the children were able to spot the word that she had changed.

They then went on to develop this language play, making up different versions of the rhyme by changing and replacing words.

- *What may the children learn about words from this activity?*

- *How could this contribute to their metalinguistic development?*

- *Why do you think Imogen chose to introduce this concept through nursery rhymes and making the children laugh?*

- *Why would the concept of a word be important in learning to read and write?*

- *Plan another activity that involves children considering and talking about words.*

SUMMARY

This chapter has outlined what is meant by literacy and identified the importance of literacy for individuals and society. It has considered how children become literate. Early literacy, it is argued, underpins later conventional literacy. Early literacy consists of a range of knowledge, skills, interests and aptitudes developed as children engage in literacy practices in their families, communities and settings, namely: becoming aware of and interested in print; learning to symbolise; having opportunities to represent their thoughts, ideas and experiences in a range of ways; engaging with the forms and functions of reading and writing; and developing metalinguistic awareness. The metaphors of an iceberg and Goodman's 'roots of literacy' are used to illustrate the relationship between early literacy and later conventional literacy. The process of engagement in early literacy is identified as emergent reading and writing. This is in accordance with the belief that becoming a reader and a writer is, predominantly, a socially embedded process.

FURTHER READING

Adams, MJ (1990) *Beginning to Read. Thinking and Learning About Print.* Cambridge, Massachusetts: MIT Press.

Brice Heath, S (1983) *Ways with Words. Language, Life and Work in Communities and Classrooms.* New York: Cambridge University Press.

Campbell, R (1995) *Reading in the Early Years Handbook.* Buckingham: Open University Press.

Goodman, Y (1986) Children coming to know literacy. In Teale, W and Sulzby, E (1986) *Emergent Literacy: Writing and Reading*. Norwood, New Jersey: Ablex Publishing Corporation.

Wells, G (1987) *The Meaning Makers: Children Learning Language and Using Language to Learn*. London: Hodder and Stoughton Educational.

WEBSITES

www.booktrust.org.uk

www.literacytrust.org.uk

13 Emergent literacy

This chapter enables you to understand:

- what is meant by emergent literacy, emergent reading and emergent writing;
- what emergent literacy looks like in practice.

Introduction

We used to think that children did not learn to read and write until they started school. We used to think that children weren't able to read until they had certain prerequisite skills such as auditory discrimination. We used to think that reading was primarily a visual process and 'reading readiness' was promoted by visual discrimination. We now know that the ability to read and write emerges gradually, with children acquiring knowledge, concepts and skills through, and about, communication almost from birth. Research that involves careful observation of children's approximations, 'scribble' writing and pretend reading, has shown us this process. We use the terms 'emergent literacy', 'emergent reading' and 'emergent writing' to describe these processes.

Nigel Hall (1997) suggests that there are four reasons for referring to this process as emergent.

1. The term indicates that the development of a child as a literacy user comes from within. It is children, supported by adults, who make sense of the print which surrounds them.

2. Emergence implies a gradual process that takes place over time.

3. Emergence focuses on the abilities that children have to make sense of the world, perceiving them as active in their learning rather than as passive recipients of knowledge.

4. Literacy only emerges if the conditions are right, so there has to be meaningful engagement with print and adults who support this for it to emerge. This also implies that early attempts at reading and writing must be respected and accepted as they are indicative of an emerging capability and need to be encouraged.

We can observe young children's engagement with literacy in their pretend reading and writing. Reading and writing behaviours that they have seen appear in their play. Emergent literacy is a way of conceptualising these reading and writing behaviours that precede and develop into conventional literacy. The concept arose from research that sought to understand the apparent, 'planfullness', (Yaden et al., 2000) behind children's unconventional writing and their early attempts at reading. It was observed that these reading and writing behaviours were an attempt to make sense of the literacy practices that they observed and were involved in. For example:

- recognising and making sense of their knowledge and understanding of print in the environment; signs, logos, captions, labels, brands;

- sharing books with adults;

- using the internet alongside adults to search for and read information;

- playing games on a computer or hand-held device that involves reading or writing;

- being apprentices to adult uses of literacy: sitting with an adult as they read, write and send emails, sending and receiving birthday cards, seeing people write and send texts, completing forms, writing lists;

- early scribbles and marks that have meaning, for example, signing a birthday card;

- using knowledge about literacy in role-play, for example, reading menus, writing orders, writing in appointment books, texting, taking telephone messages, working on a computer.

Adapted from Nutbrown (2003)

This emergent literacy perspective on early literacy shows just how much young children know about reading and writing, how they seek to make meaning of literacy practices as they grow and learn. Literacy learning therefore is seen as taking place in the home, within communities and in pre-school settings as well as in school.

THEORY FOCUS

The Jones family's culture of literacy

Johnson (2010) completed a study that documented the literacy practices of one African American family. The study showed that the family used literacy in many aspects of their everyday lives across generations, which meant that the children were apprentice to a range of literacy practices. In the study, family members recalled the ways in which literacy was used in the home as they grew up. It is important to be aware that the period recalled was prior to the widespread use of computers and mobile phones.

Literacy had a range of everyday uses in the Jones family.

- Interactional uses of literacy: letter writing and reading.

- Instrumental uses of literacy. Reading magazines for decorating ideas and craft and sewing projects. Reading recipes.

- News related uses of literacy. Reading the newspaper, national and local.

- Financial uses of literacy. Recording expenditure, budgeting, applying for loans.

- Spiritual uses of literacy. Reading the bible together each evening. Reading prayers and poems in church services. Attending Sunday School. Posters and calendars of inspirational religious sayings around the house which were often read aloud.

continued

THEORY FOCUS *continued*

- Recreational uses of literacy. Reading folk and fairy stories. Reading novels. Borrowing from the library and buying books from local shops and a yearly book fair.

- Educational uses of literacy. Supporting schoolwork, and reading with the children. Adults undertaking a degree and studying at home.

1. List the ways in which the children would regularly be alongside adults reading.

2. List the ways in which they would be alongside adults who were writing.

3. What would the children in this family be learning about literacy?

4. How may this modelled literacy practice be observed in children's play?

5. What could you learn about what children know about literacy from observing this play?

6. In what ways may children's experiences differ as they grow and learn in families today?

It is important to realise that emergent literacy does not assume that children will just come to reading and writing without any adult intervention. It is a way of understanding the ways in which children progress from their earliest engagement with literacy practices to when they become conventionally literate. It articulates the socially embedded practices that influence children's growing awareness and use of literacy. Within these everyday practices it is vital that adults mediate the learning by actively engaging with children in literacy practices, using the language of literacy, and teaching them skills that they need. For how to achieve this, see the section entitled 'What emergent literacy looks like in practice' below (page 146).

Additionally, there is clearly an intimate link between emergent literacy and phonics. Phonics is knowledge of letter sounds, and the ability to put sounds together to form words, and to separate words into letter sounds. Children will need adult support to learn phonics alongside, and as part of, their emergent reading and writing. Chapter 13 outlines in detail what phonics is and how parents and practitioners can support children's learning.

Understanding emergent reading

Emergent reading is the process of children's gradual engagement with print and its meaning. It begins with a child noticing print in their everyday lives and, through increasing sophistication in their awareness and ability to understand and make meaning of print, results in a child becoming a reader.

Environmental print

Children's earliest engagement with print is likely to be with environmental print. Environmental print is the print that children are surrounded by in their daily lives. It is often a combination of words, colours and images and can be found on packaging; as advertising; on household appliances and controls; as print on clothing, labels, branding or captions; through digital technology on phones, computers and other hand-held devices; as shop signs and logos. This print becomes meaningful to the child as they see and use it in their everyday lives.

However, this doesn't necessarily mean that children can read the print. They can recognise it and know that it carries a particular meaning but they are heavily dependent on the context of the print. Goodall (1984) found that children can recognise words when they are in their usual context, for example, a slogan on a particular item of clothing or the name of a product on a package, but are not able to read the word without these contextual clues. This is to be expected at an early stage. The important conceptual development is that print carries meaning and by reading the print we can understand that meaning. This conceptual development underpins learning to read. Additionally, environmental print can stimulate questions and discussion about reading: about why we read; about how we read; about letters and sounds; and about meanings of words, print and reading.

ACTIVITY 1

Choose one of these topics and list all the different opportunities for children to engage with environmental print:

- *buying milk at the corner shop;*
- *baking;*
- *going to the park;*
- *at a bus station, train station or airport;*
- *making breakfast;*
- *having a bath.*

1. *How would you engage a child in noticing (and reading) the print in their environment?*
2. *What may they learn about reading from this environmental print?*
3. *Why is this important when learning to read?*

Books and emergent reading

One of the most important ways in which children engage with, and learn about, reading is through storybooks. Reading books to children has a wide range of benefits (see Chapter 9), which include providing an enjoyable and authentic introduction to literacy. This is important. Learning to read needs to be more than just learning the skill of decoding text – reading, in the fullest sense, is engagement with the purposes and pleasure of reading as well as developing the skills necessary to read. Engagement with storybooks enables children to develop an understanding of the full range of knowledge, skills and affective aspects of reading. These include:

- a positive orientation to books and reading;

- an awareness of some of the functions, or purposes, of reading;

- an awareness of the forms of reading: book structure, page turning, top-to-bottom and left-to-right orientation, identification of print;

- an awareness of story structure and the language of stories;

- the development of a language for reading: letter, word, sentence, story, character and event;

- knowledge of letters (graphemes) and letter sounds (phomenes).

Sulzby and Rockafellow (2001) provide a framework that traces the development of emergent reading from the earliest engagement with storybooks through to independent reading. They observe that children's reading of books emerges initially through simple labelling and commenting based on the pictures, through a series of stages in which a child learns and refines storytelling language, to reading that uses emerging understanding of phonics and other word recognition skills to support storytelling from a book.

STAGES OF EMERGENT READING
Picture-governed attempts
Labels or responds to the pictures on each page with little or no understanding of the whole story.
Telling the story based on the picture in front of them. The story told is based on the actual story but the language of storytelling and the book is not used.
Children will tell the story using both the pictures and the language of the story that they have learned from hearing the story over and over again. Their emergent reading begins to sound like conventional reading. This indicates that the child is becoming aware of, and making a transition between, oral language and written language.
Print-governed attempts
Children will attempt to read the book using the print. This indicates that they have learned that it is the print that carries the story when adults read rather than the pictures. Some children will have remembered the story exactly and appear to read the print; others will insist on reading the print but still struggle to decode it.
Children will bring together what they know about print and what they remember of the text and pictures to read the text conventionally.

Table 13.1: Stages of emergent reading

Sulzby's (1985) work focused on emergent reading using storybooks. The same patterns can be observed in children's engagement with non-fiction texts and with rhymes and poems. Children will label and list before beginning to use some of the language of the text and eventually, from repeated exposure to the text, use what they know about print and what they remember of the text to read it conventionally.

Understanding emergent writing

Emergent writing is the process of moving from early representation to conventional writing. Very young children need to be able to symbolise – that is, to use one thing to represent another – as this is the basis of writing. This begins with children being active and communicating their ideas through engagement in sensorimotor activity. This develops through gesture (a wave for bye-bye) and the symbolic use of objects in play (a stick for a sword, a piece of fabric as a cloak, a pencil as a wand). As children grow and develop their ideas and thoughts begin to be communicated through drawing, modelling and mark-making. This representation is evidence of a child's ability to understand and use symbols. Eventually, conventional letters and words begin to emerge in what children produce. This development is gradual and emerges through engagement with writing in everyday life and routines, and through authentic experiences of literacy in settings.

Emergent writing is predominantly concerned with the process and content of writing rather than handwriting. However, as mark-making emerges and children move toward using conventional writing it is important to teach children how to hold a pencil correctly and how to form letters correctly. When opportunities arise, children can also be introduced to letter sounds (phonemes). All of this can be achieved through playing alongside children and modelling and teaching this within the context of the activity. The pedagogical approach of 'teachable moments' would be appropriate in this context (see Chapter 7).

Environmental print and mark-making

Through engagement with environmental print children become aware of letters and sounds. This requires that an adult mediates the learning by pointing out letters (graphemes) and letter sounds (phonemes). This is important in children's emergent writing because as they progress letters emerge in their writing. This may occur initially as a visual process, that is, they remember the shape of the letter, but they will eventually, with support, come to use conventional writing that makes use of patterns of letters and sounds (phonics).

Environmental print may also act as a model for children in representation and/or mark-making. For example, having seen print on a Formula One car they may use lettering on a model of a car, or they may put print or logos on clothing worn by people in their drawings.

Stages of emergent writing

As with emergent reading, a pattern of progress in emergent writing can be observed. However, it is important to remember that development is unlikely to just happen on its own, it requires both the opportunity to rehearse emerging knowledge and skill and adults to model, encourage and teach when appropriate and where necessary. Prior to children engaging in representation that approximates to conventional writing, they will need to have had sustained exposure to environmental print and have engaged in play-based activities to enable them to learn, develop and consolidate their ability to symbolise in concrete contexts (see Chapter 11).

Stages of emergent writing	
Scribbling	Emergent writing begins with first explorations in mark-making, often for purposes other then representation. These are random scribbles or marks on a page, on steamy windows, in sand, or made in mud with sticks. Very young children will use words 'drawing' and 'writing' interchangeably to describe the marks. Three-to-four-year olds have usually begun to differentiate between the two.
Mock handwriting or wavy scribble	Children produce lines of wavy scribbles in imitation of adult writing. The writing often appears on a page with drawing. This pretend writing also often appears in children's role-play within an appropriate context, such as writing an appointment in a book. Children tend to do imitation writing in large amounts, sometimes covering a page.
Mock letters	Children attempt to form alphabetic letters. These tend to be letter-like shapes that resemble conventional letters. They appear in their writing and drawing. Research has shown that that these scribbles and letter-like shapes take on the characteristics of the print in a child's culture – scribbles in Hebrew and Arabic, for example, look very different from scribbles in English (Harste et al., 1984).
Conventional letters	Children's mock letters gradually become more conventional and letters appear in what they produce. These early experiments with real letters are usually the letters in their names or close family members' names. Children often create strings of letters across a page and 'read' them as a sentence or series of sentences. The letters appear on drawings as the child's signature or as a label for the drawing. Environmental print has a particular importance at this stage as children increasingly begin to notice the detail of letters and print.
Invented spelling	Once children are comfortable with writing conventional individual letters they begin to cluster them together to make word forms. These often do not look like or sound like 'real' words. Children will often ask, 'What did I write?'
Approximated (phonetic) spelling	Children attempt to spell words based on their growing awareness of letter sounds (phonemes) and their sight vocabulary of words that they have seen repeatedly. These beginning words are often written in a random combination of upper and lower case letters, depending upon the child's knowledge and skill. Children move from spelling words using the beginning letter, to writing both beginning and final letters, to writing words with the appropriate beginning, middle and final letters.
Conventional spelling	Children's approximated spellings gradually become more and more conventional. The child's own name is usually written first.

Table 13.2: Stages of emergent writing

Source: Adapted from Project ELIPSS, Macomb Projects, Western Illinois University.

CASE STUDY

Bissex (1980): Gnys at wrk

Glenda Bissex undertook a study that documented her son's emergent writing. She became fascinated by his invented spelling and what this indicated about his understanding of writing.

Paul, her son, lived in a house full of print and frequently saw his parents reading. He had had stories read aloud to him since he was a baby and had a collection of his own books. Paul had wooden and magnetic letters and rubber letter stamps among his playthings. His

continued

145

family had not taught him letters and sounds formally but letters were frequently pointed out and referred to. Paul had watched Sesame Street *since he was three years old which, again, informally introduced him to letters and letter sounds. Paul was an only child and lived in the country which meant that he had significant periods of solitude to play and concentrate without interruption.*

Paul's first attempt at writing was a welcome home banner for his mum. It consisted of a random string of letters: zz H i D C A.

Paul was familiar with both upper and lower case letters but he chose, and preferred, to use capital letters. Bissex argues that this may be because they have visual primacy with children; capitals are more distinctive; they retain their identity even when reversed; they are used for important communication in conventional writing;

Paul's earliest attempts at writing were not attempts to spell or print letters but to communicate: the welcome home banner; a note to a friend; and a page of green letters to make his mum 'feel better'. This continued as his writing developed. The writing had a purpose, often in play, but always as an act of communication.

Paul's emergent writing ability can be observed in examples of his writing that reflect his growing awareness of print, the purposes for writing and the forms of writing. Over a period of seven months Paul made the following progress.

RUDF – Are you deaf?
PAULSTLEFNMBR – Paul's telephone number.
DOTGATNERA KOR – Don't get near a car.
I WILL TECH U TO RIT AD THES EZ HAOW – I will teach you to write and this is how.
DO NAT DSTRB GNYS AT WORK – Do not disturb genius at work.
THA. BEG. EST. HOS. EN. THA. WRALD – The biggest house in the world.
PAUL. IS GOWING. TO. RUN. A. RAWN. AND. JUMP. AND EXRSICS – Paul is going to run and run and jump and exercise.

What is important about Bissex's research is her conclusion that learning to write is a non-linear process – it doesn't follow a regular, predictable, step-by-step process. It is a process that engages with the child's interests and abilities. What was evident throughout her observations was the importance of exposure to literacy practices, embedded within everyday life, and the ongoing interaction with the adults who matched their interaction to Paul's interests and guided him towards conventional literacy.

What emergent literacy looks like in practice

Home and pre-school settings play a key role in emergent literacy. What can be observed is that the more literacy knowledge children bring to school the more likely it is that they will do well in becoming literate. The most striking implication of this is the importance of ensuring that literacy is embedded in children's lives. So what does this look like in practice? What provision and interaction best supports children's emerging literacy?

Emergent literacy in the home

We know that what parents do in the home is more important than who they are (EPPE, 2003), and in terms of literacy what parents do is of great importance. Most children will grow up with literacy practices in their homes as part of their everyday lives prior to attending a pre-school or school: talking and listening, environmental print, reading and writing. However, just being exposed to literacy practices has limited benefits for literacy development. Parents need to mediate these experiences to engage children in literacy practices. They need to draw children's attention to aspects of literacy and offer them opportunities to engage with environmental print and emergent reading and writing.

- Environmental print – children need to be encouraged to notice environmental print. It needs to be pointed out and read to them. Children need to be encouraged to 'have a go' at understanding or reading logos or print. Children's attempts at reading and understanding print in their environment need to be praised and encouraged.

- Emergent reading – children need to have books read to them and to enjoy books and stories. They need to be introduced to book structure through parents' use of the appropriate terminology and to story language and structure through hearing stories. Children need to talk about books and stories; they need time to go back through and over stories to label, discuss, comment and recall the story. They need to be encouraged to get involved in storytelling, initially through looking at the pictures and then by recalling and retelling the story. The same approach is needed for non-fiction texts, rhymes and poems – reading them to children, talking about them and encouraging retelling.

- Emergent writing – children need to be encouraged to notice when people are writing, have it explained why we write, and watch the writing process. They need to have opportunities provided for them to draw, paint, model and engage in role-play to develop their ability to symbolise and represent their ideas. As children become interested in letters and they begin to appear in what they produce, they need support in understanding letter sounds and how letters are formed. They need to hear words sounded out and watch letters being formed correctly as they are written. This teaching needs to be matched to the child's interests and ability and be done in an authentic way in the context of their play and activity.

THEORY FOCUS

Research and review: questions and tensions

A number of researchers have highlighted the fact that discussion around, and assessment of, literacy at home is dominated by school-based literacy. School-based literacy, they argue, is so dominant in how we understand literacy that it is regarded as the 'real one' and all other literacies (community literacy, literacies of popular culture, intergenerational literacy and family literacy [Knobel and Lankshear, 2003]) are regarded as less important or less valid. This, it is argued, disadvantages children who arrive in school with different literacy experiences.

continued

Purcell-Gates (1995: 9) observes a *chilling picture* of the way in which this dominance serves to block access to literacy for some children because a particular type of home-based literacy is so significant for the acquisition of school-based literacy.

Likewise, Brookner (2003) concluded that children have varying degrees of success in importing their home literacy into the classroom. She argues that, from the two cases that she studied, both of whom had considerable literacy experiences at home, only one child's assets were in the appropriate currency to be invested in the official education system.

Yaden et al.'s (2000: 437) conclusions focused on the socially embedded nature of children's writing. They comment that the studies that they reviewed highlighted the cultural and interactive basis of how children use and define literacy and note that this raises complex issues concerning *societal values and definitions of literacy, clashes of culture between home and school and differential valuing of the cultural capital that children bring to school.*

ACTIVITY **2**

Read through the theory focus above.

- *Why do you think that school literacy is so dominant?*

- *Why do some children arrive in school with different literacy experiences?*

- *Why does this mean that some children can access school learning easily while others find it more difficult?*

- *What does this mean for provision in pre-school settings? Think carefully about this question. Does it mean that pre-schools should exist to prepare children for school or do they have a different purpose? What are the benefits and difficulties with each of these approaches?*

Emergent literacy in settings

In contrast to homes and communities, there are very few naturally occurring opportunities for authentic literacy experiences in settings and schools. Therefore, practitioners need to:

- provide a literate environment in which children can engage in contextualised literacy practices;

- adopt a pedagogical approach that models, encourages and teaches literacy.

A positive literacy-learning environment needs to be print rich. There needs to be extensive use of labelling, captions and instructions. Books need to be readily available and regularly read to the children. Opportunities for literacy in routines need to be used to engage children in literacy practices, for example, self-registration, sign-up sheets for computer use and labelled boxes for tidying up.

Preparing the classroom environment to promote literacy during play

Morrow (1990) explored spatial and affective aspects of learning environments that promote literacy during play. She cites evidence to suggest that children in well-defined settings, that included smaller partitioned spaces, exhibited more engaged and exploratory play behaviours and more social interaction and cooperation. She also proposes that storing equipment on open shelving rather than in boxes was found to affect access to, and use of, materials. She observed that the use of book corners increased when practitioners designed attractive, accessible areas stocked with a large and varied selection of books and other reading materials, as well as other opportunities for literacy such as storyboards, taped stories and puppets.

Practitioners need to provide for children to engage in representation through drawing, modelling, mark-making and role-play and to plan activities and experiences that enable children to engage in emergent reading and writing. This requires that careful thought is given to how literacy can be incorporated into activities in an authentic, contextualised way. This is important. Children need to learn about why we read and write as well as how we read and write. Play that mimics real uses of literacy communicates why we need to read and write. For example, in a role-play take-away pizza shop children can engage with a range of environmental print in the shop and on the boxes and delivery vehicles, read the menus and write down orders and addresses using their emergent literacy skills.

Practitioners also need to get involved in the activities alongside children to:

* encourage reading and writing: playing alongside children and getting involved in reading and writing will show children how literacy is part of the activity and encourage them to incorporate this in their play;

* model reading and writing: sounding out words when reading and allowing children to see writing happening will model the processes of reading and writing;

* teach literacy: where appropriate practitioners should teach children letter sounds (phonemes) and how to form letters correctly. Using 'teachable moments' is an appropriate pedagogical strategy for modelling reading and writing and teaching children about letter formation and letter sounds during play-based activities.

Teachable moments: these are moments when a practitioner notices that a child is ready to learn something and seizes the moment to teach the child, moving the child's learning forward. It relies on the practitioner knowing the child well and being able to notice and use moments as they arise to engage with the child at an appropriate level to enhance their learning.

CASE STUDY

Authentic uses of literacy in the nursery: using emergent reading and writing in daily routines

Each day two children in the nursery collected a list of the drinks that all the staff, parents, volunteers and students wanted mid-morning. The children and the teacher wrote a list of all the names of the adults each day on a grid on a whiteboard. The children's contribution varied according to their ability. Some children observed the teacher writing the list. Other children were able to identify the initial sound of the adult's name and observe the teacher writing it down. Some children were able to sound out parts of the adult's names and observe the teacher writing it down. Other children wrote the initial sound of the adult's name, and some were able to make phonetically plausible attempts at sounding out the adults' names and writing them in a list.

The children then went to each adult in turn and asked what they would like to drink. This was recorded on the list. The way in which this was done was dependent upon individual children's ability. Each adult encouraged the children to find their name on the list as they came to ask for their drinks order. Some of the children needed the name to be pointed out and sounded out. Some of the children were able to find names using the initial sound and letter; others could find names by sounding out letters and blending them into words.

For some of the children the adults wrote their request next to their name, observed by the child. Other children were able to make a mark in a grid according to the adult's choice. Some children were able to write the initial sound of the adult's choice and some children wrote the request in a phonetically plausible way next to the appropriate name.

The children collected the necessary information and hung it on a hook next to the kitchen door, ready for the staff to make the drinks.

- *List the different ways in which practitioners involved children in emergent reading and writing in this daily routine.*

- *What do you think this communicated to children about the purposes of literacy?*

- *What do you think children learned about the forms of literacy?*

- *Why did the practitioners use a daily routine to teach literacy?*

- *Why do you think practitioners did different things with different children?*

- *What would you need to know about individual children to enable you to differentiate your interaction in these ways?*

SUMMARY

This chapter has explained what is meant by emergent reading and writing, and identified what this looks like in practice. Stages of emergent reading and writing are outlined. The importance of engagement with environmental print and storybook reading are highlighted as significant in emergent reading. The importance of opportunities for developing the ability to symbolise, to represent ideas, thoughts and experiences through drawing, modelling and mark-making, and to engage in contextualised uses of writing are identified as important in emergent writing. The use of 'teachable moments' is identified as an appropriate pedagogical strategy for modelling reading and writing and teaching children about letter formation and letter sounds during play-based activities. Case studies and research evidence are used to support your understanding.

FURTHER READING

Adams, MJ (1990) *Beginning to Read. Thinking and Learning About Print*. Cambridge, Massachusetts: MIT Press.

Bissex, G (1980) *Gnys at wrk. A Child Learns to Write and Read*. London: Harvard University Press.

Campbell, R (1995) *Reading in the Early Years Handbook*. Buckingham: Open University Press.

Goouch, K and Lambirth, A (2011) *Teaching Early Reading and Phonics. Creative Approaches to Early Literacy*. London: SAGE.

Hall, N (1997) *The Emergence of Literacy*. Sevenoaks: Hodder and Stoughton.

Kress, G (1997) *Before Writing. Rethinking Pathways to Literacy*. London: Routledge.

Teale, W and Sulzby, E (1986) *Emergent Literacy: Writing and Reading*. Norwood, New Jersey: Ablex Publishing Corporation.

Wells, G (1987) *The Meaning Makers: Children Learning Language and Using Language to Learn*. London: Hodder and Stoughton Educational.

14 Phonics in the early years

This chapter enables you to understand:

- what is meant by phonics (including current guidance on teaching reading in school and tensions and debates around teaching reading);
- phonics and the early years (including what comes before phonics and teaching phonics within an early years pedagogical approach).

Introduction

English is an alphabetic writing system. That means that we use an alphabetic code to compose texts (write) and interpret texts (read). This is in contrast to a logographic system, such as Chinese, which uses symbols to communicate meaning, with each symbol representing an idea. An alphabetic system uses letters to represent individual spoken sounds, and groups these letters together to form words. Becoming a reader and a writer depends on the ability to recognise and decode these letters, words and sentences to make meaning. Teaching reading and writing in settings and schools requires consideration of how we teach this to children. This issue is not straightforward: there are different and strongly held views on how to achieve this.

What is phonics?

Phonics is a method of teaching reading based on learning letter sounds and their corresponding letters, and blending and segmenting them into words. It is based on the alphabetic principle that once you have learned the alphabet you can read and write unfamiliar words.

Phonics requires that children learn:

- *phonemes* – the smallest units of sound. This may be a letter sound /p/ or /r/, or it may be a sound that is written as a combination of letters /sh/ as in sh<u>oe</u>, /oo/ as in b<u>oo</u>k, /igh/ as in l<u>igh</u>t, /ough/ as in b<u>ough</u>t. The English alphabet has 26 letters and 40+ phonemes;

- *graphemes* – the letter or combination of letters that represent a phoneme;

- *grapheme – phoneme correspondence* – which letter or letters correspond to a particular sound;

- *to blend* – to combine phonemes to make words;

- *to segment* – to separate words into phonemes.

In order to become a reader and a writer in English, we need an understanding of the alphabetic code. For most children phonics is the most efficient way of accessing print. Once they have learned the alphabetic code, they are able to use this skill to work out words that they have not come across before. However, it is important to realise that phonics is only a skill: it is a skill that enables access to other things. Learning phonics is not an end in itself; it is one part of a process of becoming a reader and a writer. A straightforward analogy is one of learning ball skills. Ball skills are learned to enable you to play sports well. You do not learn ball skills as an end in itself; to learn ball skills, they are learned to enable something else. Similarly, you do not learn phonics to learn phonics. Phonics is an enabling skill that is one part of becoming a reader and a writer.

It is also important to be aware that, whilst most children will respond to using a phonic approach to reading, some children will need a different approach to enable them to become literate. The ultimate aim is for all children to learn to read and write so for some children a different approach, or a different emphasis, may be necessary.

While there is general acceptance that learning the alphabetic code is an important part of reading and writing, how and when we teach phonics in our settings and schools is the subject of intense debate. This is due, in part, to the current commitment to using only one, particular approach to teaching phonics in settings and schools: systematic synthetic phonics.

Systematic synthetic phonics

Systematic synthetic phonics is an approach to teaching phonics. It is the approach embedded in the government's current guidance on the teaching of reading. The approach adopts the Simple View of Reading, which identifies two processes in reading: recognising words and understanding text. In this model these two aspects of reading are separate and must be actively taught as different skills that underpin the ability to read words (word recognition skills) and the ability to understand sentences and texts (language comprehension). A good reader will have both good word recognition and good language comprehension skills. Language comprehension is developed in the early years through sustained engagement in spoken language and with books. Synthetic phonics is a way of teaching word recognition skills.

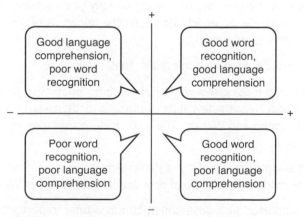

Figure 14.1: The Simple View of Reading

Johnston and Watson (2007: 35) explain synthetic phonics thus:

> *In the early days of learning to read children need to learn how to recognise printed words. Once they have acquired some decoding skill, children can make sense of simple written sentences ... when children can recognise and spell words with ease, they will be able to concentrate on understanding what they read, and produce good written work. The role of synthetic phonics teaching, therefore, is to establish children's word recognition and spelling skills early on in their schooling, as a basis for good reading comprehension and writing skills.*

The guidance for settings and schools on teaching reading in this way specifically states that children should not use unreliable strategies when dealing with unfamiliar words, such as looking at pictures or looking at the first letters and guessing the word. Instead, that decoding through the word should be taught and strongly encouraged.

There are a number of identifiable features of a synthetic phonics programme.

- Letters and sounds (grapheme – phoneme correspondence) are taught in a defined incremental sequence.

- As soon as they are introduced they are used to blend (synthesise) into words.

- Words that are not phonetically regular, and so cannot be 'sounded out' are termed 'tricky words' and children are encouraged to focus on the decodable or phonetically regular elements of these words, even if it is only the initial letter.

- It advocates an early start to reading decodable text.

- Once you have selected a programme to follow you should follow it. This consistency is called 'fidelity to the system'.

Current guidance on using synthetic phonics can be found in the document *Letters and Sounds* (DfES, 2007). This is based on the outcomes of *The Independent Review of the Teaching of Reading* (DfES, 2006). In the review, Rose (DfES 2006: 19) concluded that, within a context of rich language provision in schools and settings, synthetic phonics is the form of systematic phonic work that offers the vast majority of beginners the best route to becoming skilled readers. This conclusion was accepted by the government and therefore guidance on the teaching of reading in early years settings and schools advocates a systematic synthetic approach. However, the adoption of a single system across the education system is controversial.

Advocates of systematic synthetic phonics claim that:

- it is the quickest and most effective way of teaching phonics in that children, shortly after starting school, learn a few letter sounds and then start to sound and blend straight away (Johnston and Watson, 2007). They claim that new letter sounds are then learned quite rapidly;

- studies show that synthetic phonics is a particularly effective method of teaching phonics, especially for children from areas of deprivation (Johnston and Watson, 2005);

- this view was supported in a government-commissioned report into the teaching of reading (DfES, 2006).

Others (Dombey, 2010; Goouch and Lambirth, 2011; Goswami, 2002, 2005; Hynds, 2007) express concern. They claim that:

- English is not written in a consistently phonic way, and has an inconsistent orthography (the conventional spelling system of a language), and therefore this demands variety and complexity in its methods of teaching;

- reading phonetically is not the same as reading. Reading is not just pronouncing written words. Children who become avid and accomplished readers focus on making sense. We need to ensure that our central concern is with learning to read for meaning;

- engagement in reading has a significant impact on progress in reading and synthetic phonics focuses on skills not engagement;

- synthetic phonics is a narrow, limited, 'dry' skills-based method of teaching something as rich and potentially engaging as reading (and writing);

- experience and research tells us that children are diverse in terms of personality and the linguistic and emotional experience that they bring to the classroom: a one-size-fits-all approach cannot meet these diverse needs.

Other approaches to the teaching of reading and writing
As well as synthetic phonics there are other ways to teach children to read.

Some argue that these methods are not necessarily incompatible with one another (Hall, 2009), just that they are different ways of achieving the same end: to enable children to read and write. However, there are strong critics of a 'mixed-methods' approach who claim that the evidence on teaching reading effectively points towards a single systematic synthetic approach.

Analytic phonics
Analytic phonics introduces children to whole words and teaches them to analyse them in their component parts. This system stresses the importance of larger units of onsets and rimes as well as phonemes (Wyse and Styles, 2007). Onset is the part of the syllable before the vowel. Rime is the part of the syllable from the first vowel onwards: s/un, sh/eep, p/en (Goouch and Lambirth, 2011).

Critics of this approach claim that it is not as effective as synthetic phonics. In the study that strongly influenced the Rose Review the researchers compared the use of synthetic and analytic phonics. Their results showed that the children using analytic phonics made progress commensurate with their chronological age, but children taught through synthetic phonics made significantly better progress (Johnston and Watson, 2005).

However, the study itself has been criticised for poor research design and bias towards synthetic phonics (Goswami, 2007, Wyse and Styles, 2007).

Look and say
With this approach children learn to recognise whole words or sentences rather than individual sounds. Pedagogical approaches in a look and say approach include sounding out a word for children who then say the whole word, and using flashcards for word recognition. In this approach children are encouraged to use pictures and context to help predict words.

Critics of this approach argue that it does not enable children to have ways of working out words when they come across unfamiliar words. Therefore, it is not an efficient way of learning the vast number of words needed to read and write effectively as it relies on, and requires, a large sight memory of words and/or patterns in words.

In conclusion, systematic synthetic phonics is the approach that is currently used in settings and schools. It is the phonics teaching approach that is embedded in *Letters and Sounds* (DfES, 2007) guidance for settings and schools on the teaching of reading. This is controversial for the reasons outlined above. The debate about how to teach children to read is a long and fiercely contested debate, with strongly held positions on both sides.

Letters and sounds

Letters and Sounds (DfES, 2007) is the government's guidance on the teaching of phonics in settings and schools. It is a two-phase teaching programme.

- Phase one concentrates on activities to promote speaking and listening, phonological awareness and oral blending and segmenting.

- Phase two contains six focuses on phonic work based on a systematic synthetic phonics approach.

Foundation Stage is phase one. The programme is designed as one part of the provision for language and literacy.

Phase one lists seven aspects of early phonics and a series of activities to develop each one. The aspects are:

1. General sound discrimination – environmental sounds.

2. General sound discrimination – instrumental sounds.

3. General sound discrimination – body percussion.

4. Rhyme and rhythm.

5. Alliteration.

6. Voice sounds.

7. Oral blending and segmenting.

There is an expectation that most children will be working toward aspect seven by the end of the Foundation Stage.

As well as this provision for phonics, practitioners are encouraged to enjoy and share books with children, to listen and encourage talking, and to provide good models of spoken English. Music and rhyme are identified as important and play-based, language-rich provision encouraged.

Phonics and the early years

The debate about how best to teach children the formal skills of reading and writing conventionally sits at the cusp of early years. Most children in early years will be at the stage of learning and developing early literacy knowledge and skills and using these emergently in their play, and this approach in the early years is less controversial. Indeed, it is generally agreed that there are a range of early experiences that are highly significant in enabling children to become literate. In Chapter 12 the metaphors of an iceberg and roots were used to illustrate the importance of early experiences, pointing to the fact that later, formal literacy teaching requires strong underpinnings. So, because a strong foundation is so significant for later learning, it is important that in early years we focus on building this strong foundation. We need to retain our play-based, contextualised and emergent approach to early literacy, and resist the trickle-down pressure to teach formal knowledge and skills in a formal way too soon.

Therefore, developing children's positive orientation to reading and writing, and the knowledge and skills that will enable them to become conventionally literate is an important part of provision and pedagogy in the early years. To achieve this, early years provision must include frequent, meaningful and rich experiences with literacy, and a pedagogical approach that engages children and uses this engagement to develop a positive orientation and teach necessary early knowledge and skills. So what comes before the formal teaching of phonics? And how do we begin the move into phonics for children who are ready to learn, while maintaining a strong early years pedagogical approach?

What comes before phonics?

Children need wide experience of language and literacy before they can meaningfully access the teaching of letter sounds and their correspondence to letters. Clearly, children will see letters and hear people using letters sounds, which is good, but learning in children's earliest years needs to focus on wider aspects of literacy to provide a meaningful context for later phonic teaching.

Many of the aspects of provision and pedagogy listed below appear throughout this book. This is indicative of the approach to teaching and learning in early years. Learning in the early years is viewed as holistic and integrated rather than separated out as 'subjects' or 'lessons', therefore one activity or experience can potentially develop a wide range of knowledge and skill. This section will detail how the activities contribute to learning phonics.

Talk and listening

From their earliest days young children are tuning into language. They are sensitive and responsive to voices and other sounds around them. Very quickly, young children, begin to discriminate between sounds. As children grow and learn they further engage with sound and listening through language play, including learning rhymes, and through music and song. This tuning into the language is an important part of later phonics learning.

Children need lots of time and experience of language for them to develop and refine these skills. Additionally, talk and listening develop children's vocabulary and understanding of grammar, teaches them about patterns and meaning in language and so develops their language knowledge and comprehension. Talk is vital to literacy development, as has been explored widely in this book. So settings must enable children to talk and listen through provision that promotes talk and through a pedagogical approach that actively engages children in talking and listening.

Books and reading

Access to, and engagement with, books is crucial in developing children's understanding of reading. It enables children to begin to understand the purpose of reading and print. This places phonic learning in a meaningful context and then becomes evident in children's emergent reading and writing as they explore the ways in which we communicate meaning in print.

Play-based experiences that communicate the purposes of reading and writing

Provision for play in the Early Years needs to include opportunities for children to use their emergent reading and writing in meaningful contexts. Practitioners need to engage with children during these activities to model the functions and forms of reading and writing, including phonics. Appropriate pedagogical strategies include commentary, modelling and using opportunities that arise to teach specific knowledge and skill (teachable moments). A case study in Chapter 13 (page 150) shows this in practice.

Phonological awareness

Prior to being able to hear and meaningfully understand the subtle sounds that are letter sounds, children need lots of experience in tuning into language and sound. This ability to listen carefully, to be sensitive to sound and hear and notice differences is called phonological awareness. Having lots of experience of rhyme and alliteration, language play, song and music is vital to children developing a good phonological awareness.

CASE STUDY

Supporting children's phonological development

The playgroup had set up their role-play area as a snowy landscape following the children's interest in and discussions about the television documentary Frozen Planet. *Just like on the TV the children wanted music and sound effects in their landscape. So, as one of the planned activities, staff and children listened to a range of different music on YouTube. The children had to decide which pieces of music best reflected the snowy landscape and record their preferences on a grid. The ones that most children preferred were sourced and put together as a soundscape by the staff and used the following week in the role-play area. Additionally, children recorded sound effects using their voices, environmental sounds and musical instruments. These were played alongside the music in the landscape.*

- *In what ways does this activity support children's phonological development?*

- *How else could you use this snowy-landscape music and sound effects to further develop children's phonological sensitivity?*

Metalinguistic awareness

Metalinguistic awareness is the ability to reflect on language as an object (Sulzby and Teale, 1991). In order to be able to understand and use the language associated with phonics children need to learn the appropriate words and concepts. For example, they need significant experience of hearing the word 'letter' alongside seeing a concrete example of a 'letter' to enable them to begin to understand what we mean when we talk about a letter. Children need to learn these words and concepts through their use in meaningful contexts. For example, when children hang up their coats pointing out their name on the peg and saying, *That's your peg. I know because I can read your name. Look, the first letter 'R' makes the sound 'R', for Ruby*. Or, when writing a name of a child's painting saying, *These are the letter sounds in your name G-e-o-r-g-i-a* as you write them on the painting. Through these small interactions that are repeated over and over and over again children develop concepts and the associated language for those concepts.

THEORY FOCUS

Metalinguistic awareness: understanding the word 'word'

Three-year-old Phoebe was asked, *what is the difference between these words: table – tables, cow – cows*.

Her response, after some thought, was 'a table doesn't have a head'.

There could be a number of reasons for this response, one of which is that she does not yet have a concept or the language to know what a 'word' is. Phoebe understood the question to be about a table and a cow (the referent) whereas the question was about the *word* table and the *word* cow. But the concept of a word and the word 'word' does not yet exist for Phoebe, just the referent (the thing that was being referred to). So her response was based on the difference between a cow and table, so 'a table doesn't have a head' is a well-considered and appropriate response.

Karmiloff-Smith et al. (1994) explored this notion of children's understanding of a word. In their study, children listened to a story in which the narrator paused and asked the children to repeat 'the last word' or 'the last thing' that she had said. Their results showed that children aged four and a half to five years old were able to differentiate between 'word' and 'thing'.

How do we teach phonics within an early years pedagogical approach?

Some children within the early years will be ready to begin learning phonics. They will be interested in the print in books and engage with it in their play, and letters will have begun to appear in their drawing and emergent writing. Clearly, good practice is that we engage with the child's stage of development, and so, in this instance, support their development of phonemic awareness.

Phonemic awareness is part of phonological development but refers specifically to a child's sensitivity to, and awareness of, the structure of words. It requires a level of analysis of the constituent sounds in a word so is more than just auditory discrimination. This is an important distinction. Reading requires readers to be able to notice and reflect on words and letters and their correspondence to sound. So children need to be able to hear and begin to develop this sensitivity through engagement and interest in print supported by adults. This enables them to progress from shallow to deep awareness (Stanovich, 1992).

Teaching phonics at this stage needs to be achieved within a child-centred, play-based, early years pedagogical approach. Phonics can be taught in context and through children's play-based activity using different pedagogical strategies.

In the earliest stages as children become interested in the detail of print, commentary can be used to introduce letter names and sounds, and to model blending sounds into words. For example, sounding out a child's name as it is written on a painting, identifying initial sounds on labelled cups at snack time so a child can identify which is theirs, writing lists of shopping for baking activities with the children and modelling blending sounds into words as you write the list. This process of articulating letter sounds and blending them into words supports children's phonemic awareness.

As children's emergent reading and writing develop direct teaching of letter names and sounds can be employed. This requires that practitioners are alert to and pick up on what children are interested in and what they produce, and use these 'teachable moments' as they arise. For example, take the case of a child who has made a model and wants to put it on show with a caption. The practitioner would share the writing with the child, encouraging the child to write what they knew and supporting their learning of letter sounds and letter formation by sounding out and modelling formation of letters and the structure of writing.

It may also be appropriate, depending on children's interests and engagement with print, to plan activities with the intention of teaching some sounds. It may be advisable to look at the pattern for teaching sounds in *Letters and Sounds* (DfES, 2007). What is important is that these activities are play-based, involve active learning and are meaningful for the child, for example, working within a theme of pirates, reading a book about finding treasure then doing a treasure hunt in the sand. The children can find the treasure and put it in a box labelled with the appropriate initial letter. This treasure can then be used to retell the story and/or in role-play. The focus in the initial and follow-up activities, and the storytelling, would be to teach the planned sounds.

ACTIVITY **1**

Consider the following activities in an early years setting:

- *routines;*
- *planning and setting up provision;*

---

continued

- *during activities;*

- *planned activities and experiences.*

How would you incorporate teaching phonics to children during these activities?

Consider:

- *young children who are becoming interested in print but not yet engaged in emergent reading and writing;*

- *children who are beginning to engage in the earliest stages of emergent reading and writing;*

- *children who are beginning to learn some phonic sounds.*

See Chapter 12 for more detailed explanations of these stages.

This highly contextualised and child-centred approach to early literacy will enable most children to engage with the more formal literacy teaching in school because they will have the necessary foundations on which to build. However, for some children it will be necessary for an emergent, child-centred approach to continue beyond the start of statutory schooling. Continuing this pedagogical approach will ensure that phonics teaching remains relevant and appropriate, because like all effective learning and teaching, it must start from what a child knows and can do.

SUMMARY

This chapter identifies that English is an alphabetic writing system and so learning to write and to read requires knowledge of that system. Phonics is discussed as a method of teaching the alphabetic code. The current system for teaching phonics in schools is identified and tensions and debates around this system outlined. Phonics teaching in the early years is considered, firstly the knowledge and skills that come before phonics and then, as children grow and learn, how they can develop phonemic awareness within established early years pedagogical practice. Examples of practice are woven throughout the chapter to enable you to envisage what the teaching of phonics in the early years looks like in practice.

FURTHER READING

Adams, MJ (1990) *Beginning to Read. Thinking and Learning About Print.* Cambridge, Massachusetts: MIT Press.

Bissex, G (1980) *Gnys at wrk. A Child Learns to Write and Read.* London: Harvard University Press.

Dombey, H (2010) *Teaching Reading: What the Evidence Says.* UKLA. Available at www.ukla.org

Campbell, R (1995) *Reading in the Early Years Handbook.* Buckingham: Open University Press.

Goouch, K and Lambirth, A (2011) *Teaching Early Reading and Phonics. Creative Approaches to Early Literacy*. London: SAGE.

Johnston, R and Watson, J (2007) *Teaching Synthetic Phonics*. Exeter: Learning Matters.

Jolliffe, W, Waugh, D and Carss, A (2012) *Teaching Systematic Synthetic Phonics in Primary Schools*. Exeter: Learning Matters.

Millard, E (1997) *Differently Literate: Boys, Girls and the Schooling of Literacy*. Abingdon: Routledge.

Whitehead, M (2010) *Language and Literacy in the Early Years 0–7*, 4th Edition. London. SAGE.

WEBSITES

www.literacytrust.org.uk

www.UKLA.org

www.piecorbett.org.uk

www.rrf.org.uk

References

Allen, G (2011) *Early Intervention. The Next Steps*. Available at: www.dwp.gov.uk/docs/early-intervention. next-steps.pdf (accessed 05.05.12)

Allen, G and Duncan Smith I (2008) *Early Intervention: Good Parents, Great Kids, Better Citizens*. The Smith Institute: Centre for Social Justice.

Bissex, G (1980) *Gnys at wrk. A Child Learns to Write and Read*. London: Harvard University Press.

Blake, Q (1990) *ALL JOIN IN*. London: Random House Children's Books.

Booktrust: www.booktrust.org.uk (accessed 05.05.12)

Bowlby, J (1953) Childcare and the Growth of Love. London: Pengiun.

Brice Heath, S (1983) *Ways with Words. Language, Life and Work in Communities and Classrooms*. New York: Cambridge University Press.

Bronfenbrenner, U (1979) *The Ecology of Human Development*. Cambridge: MA: Harvard University Press.

Brookner, L (2003) Five on the first of December. What we can learn from case studies of early childhood literacy. *Journal of Early Childhood Literacy*, 2(3), 291–313.

Bruce, T and Meggitt, C (2002) *Childcare and Education*. Abingdon: Hodder Arnold.

Bryant, PE, Bradley, L, Maclean, M and Crossland, J (1989) Nursery rhymes, phonological skills and reading. *Journal of Child Language*, 16, 407–428. Available at: http://journals.cambridge.org/action/displayAbstract?fromPage=online&aid=4234332 (accessed 05.05.12)

Bullock Report (1975) *A Language for Life*. Available at: www.educationengland.org.uk/documents/bullock (accessed 15.02.12).

Burman, E (2008) *Deconstructing Developmental Psychology*. London: Routledge.

Chambers (1991) in Goouch, K and Lambirth, A (2011) *Teaching Early Reading and Phonics*. Creative Approaches to Early Literacy. London: Sage.

Clark, A and Moss, P (2001) *Listening to Young Children. The Mosaic Approach*. National Children's Bureau.

Close (2004) *Television and Language Development in the Early Years. A Review of the Literature*. National Literacy Trust. Available at www.literacytrust.org.uk/assets/0000/0429/TV_early_years_2004.pdf (accessed 05.05.12)

Cole, B (1996) *Princess Smartypants*. London: Puffin.

Cope, B and Kalantzis, M (2000) *Multiliteracies. Literacy Learning and the Design of Social Futures*. London: Routledge.

Cremin, L, Mottram, M, Collins, C and Powell, S (2008) *Teachers as Readers: Building Communities of Readers*. UKLA. Available at: www.ukla.org/downloads/teachers_as_readers.pdf (accessed 05.05.12)

Cremin, T, Bearne, E, Goodwin, P and Mottram, M (2008) Primary Teachers as Readers. *English in Education* 42 (1): 1–16.

Crystal, D (1997) Climbing the Language Mountain. Early Years of Schooling Conference. Keynote speech. Available at: www.davidcrystal.com/DC_articles/Education7.pdf (accessed 05.05.12).

Crystal, D (1998) *Language Play*. London: Penguin.

Czikszentmihalyi, M (2008) *The Psychology of Optimal Experience*. London: Harper.

Dahlberg, G, Moss, P and Pence, A (1999) *Beyond Quality in Early Childhood Education and Care*. London: Routledge.

DCSF (2008) *Inclusion development programme. Supporting children with speech, language and communication needs: Guidance for practitioners in the Early Years Foundation Stage*. Nottingham: DCSF Publications.

Desrochers, S, Morosette, P and Ricard, M (1995) Two perspectives on pointing in infancy. In National Literacy Trust (2010) *Highlights from a Literature Review Prepared for the Face to Face research project*. Funded by the Department for Education's Children, Young People and Families Grant Programme. Available at: www.literacytrust.org.uk/assets/0000/6770/F2F_literature_highlights.pdf

DfES (2006) *Independent Review of the Teaching of Early Reading*. London: DfES. Available at: www.education.gov.uk/publications/standard/publicationDetail/Page1/DFES-0201-2006 (accessed 05.05.12).

DfES (2007) *Letters and Sounds. Principles and Practice of High Quality Phonics*. Available at: www.education.gov.uk/publications/standard/publicationDetail/Page1/DFES-00281-2007 (accessed 05.05.12).

Dolya, G (2010) *Vygotsky in Action in the Early Years*. London: David Fulton.

Dombey, H (2010) *Teaching Reading: What the Evidence Says*. UKLA: Available at: www.ukla.org (accessed 05.05.12).

Donaldson, J and Scheffler, A (2000) *Monkey Puzzle*. London: Macmillan Children's Books.

Duffy, CA (2007) *The Hat*. London: Faber.

Dury, R and Robertson, L (2008) *Stages of Early Bilingual Learning*. Available at: www.naldic.org.uk (accessed 05.05.12).

ECAT (2011) *Every Child A Talker*. Available at: http://dera.ioe.ac.uk/748/ (accessed 15.02.12).

EPPE (2003) Sylva, K, Meluish, E, Sammons, P, Siraj-Blatchford, I, Taggart, B and Elliot K (2003) *Effective Provision of Pre-School (EPPE) Project: Findings from the Pre-School Period*. Available at: http://eppe.ioe.ac.uk/eppe/eppefindings.htm (accessed 15.02.12).

Felix, M (2003) *The Boat (Mouse Books)*. The Creative Company.

Gilligan, C (1982) *In a Different Voice. Psychological Theory and Women's Development*. London: Harvard University Press.

Gombert, E (1992) *Metalinguistic Development*. Chicago: University of Chicago Press.

Goodall, M (1984) Can four year olds 'read' words in the environment? *Reading Teacher*, 37(6), 478–489.

Goodman, Y (1986) *Children coming to know literacy*. In Teale, W and Sulzby, E (1986) *Emergent Literacy: Writing and Reading*. Norwood, New Jersey: Ablex Publishing Corporation.

Goouch, K and Lambirth, A (2011) *Teaching Early Reading and Phonics. Creative Approaches to Early Literacy*. London: SAGE.

Goswami, U (2002; 2005; 2007) in Goouch, K and Lambirth, A (2011) *Teaching Early Reading and Phonics. Creative approaches to Early Literacy*. London: SAGE.

Hall, N (1997) *The Emergence of Literacy*. Sevenoaks: Hodder and Stoughton.

Hall, N (2009) in Goouch, K and Lambirth, A (2011) *Teaching Early Reading and Phonics. Creative Approaches to Early Literacy*. London: SAGE.

Hansen, OH (2010) Usage based language acquisition in the Danish Crèche. Paper presented at the OMEP World Conference, 11–13 August 2010. (search Google scholar: Hansen Usage based Danish creche)

Harste, JC, Woodward, VA and Burke, CL (1984) *Language Stories and Literacy Lessons*. Portsmouth, NH: Heinemann.

Hart, B and Risley, TR (1995) *Meaningful Differences in the Everyday Experience of Young American Children* (revised January 2003). Baltimore, MD: Brookes Publishing.

Hoff, E (2006) How social contexts support and shape language development. *Developmental Review*, 26 (1): 55–88.

Hurtado, N, Marchman, VA and Fernald, A (2008) Does input influence uptake? *Developmental Science*, 11(6) F31-F39. In Saxton, M (2001) *Child Language. Acquisition and Development*. London: SAGE.

Hynds, J (2007) in Goouch, K and Lambirth, A (2011) *Teaching Early Reading and Phonics. Creative Approaches to Early Literacy*. London: SAGE.

Iverson, JM and Goldin-Meadow, S (2005) Gesture paves the way for language development. American Psychological Society, 16 (5), 367–371. In *National Literacy Trust (2010) Highlights from a Literature Review Prepared for the Face to Face Research Project*. Funded by the Department for Education's Children, Young People and Families Grant Programme. Available at: www.literacytrust.org.uk/talk_to_your_body/policy_research/1711_research_gesture_paves_the_way_for_language_development (accessed 05.05.12).

James, A and Prout, A (1997) *Constructing and Reconstructing Childhood* (2nd Edition). London: Falmer.

Jarman, E (2007) *Communication Friendly Spaces. Improving Speaking and Listening Skills in the Early Years Foundation Stage*. Nottingham: Basic Skills Agency. Available at: www.elizabethjarmantraining.co.uk/index.php?option=com_content&view=article&id=2&Itemid=6

Johnson, AS (2010) The Jones family's culture of literacy. *The Reading Teacher*, 64 (1): 33–44.

Johnston, R and Watson, J (2005) *The Effects of Synthetic Phonics Teaching on Reading and Spelling Attainment, A Seven Year Longitudinal Study*. Scottish Executive Education Department.

Johnston, R and Watson, J (2007) *Teaching Synthetic Phonics*. Exeter: Learning Matters.

Karmiloff-Smith, A, Grant, J, Sims, K, Jones, MC and Cuckle, P (1994) Rethinking metalinguistic awareness: representing and accessing knowledge about what counts as a word. *Cognition*, 58 (2): 197–219.

Knobel, M and Lankshear, C (2003) *New Literacies*. Milton Keynes: Open University Press.

Kress, G (1997) *Before Writing. Rethinking Pathways to Literacy*. London: Routledge.

Lankshear, C (1997) In Marsh, J (2000) Teletubby Tales: Popular Culture in the Early Years Literacy Curriculum. *Contemporary Issues in Early Childhood*, 1 (2): 119–133.

Locke, A, Ginsborg and Peers, I (2002) Development and disadvantage: implications for the early years and beyond. *International Journal of Language and Communication Disorders*, 3–15.

Lockwood, M (2011) *Bringing Poetry Alive*. London: SAGE.

Luke (1993) *The Social Construct of Literacy in the Primary School*. Melbourne: Macmillan.

Marsh, J (2000) Teletubby Tales: Popular Culture in the Early Years Literacy Curriculum. *Contemporary Issues in Early Childhood*, 1 (2): 119–133.

Marsh, J and Millard, E (2000) *Literacy and Popular Culture. Using Children's Culture in the Classroom*. London: SAGE.

McCaughrean, G (2007) *The Kite Rider*. Oxford: Oxford University Press.

Moore, M and Wade, B (2003) Bookstart; A Qualitative Evaluation. *Educational Review*, 55 (1): 3–13.

Morrow, LM (1990) Preparing the classroom environment to promote literacy during play. *Early Childhood Research Quarterly*, 5: 537–554.

Munsch, R and Martchenko, M (2009) *The Paperbag Princess*. Toronto: Annick Press.

National Literacy Trust (2010) *Highlights from a Literature Review Prepared for the Face to Face Research Project*. Funded by the Department for Education's Children, Young People and Families Grant Programme. Available at: www.literacytrust.org.uk/assets/0000/6770/F2F_literature_highlights.pdf (accessed 06.05.12).

National Scientific Council on the Developing Child (2005) Excessive Stress Disrupts the Architecture of the Developing Brain: Working Paper 3. Available at: www.developingchild.net (accessed 06.05.12).

National Scientific Council on the Developing Child (2008) Mental Health Problems in Early Childhood can Impair Learning and Behavior for Life: Working Paper 6. Available at: www.developingchild.net (accessed 06.05.12).

National Scientific Council on the Developing Child (2011) Building the Brain's Air Traffic Control System: How Early Experiences Shape the Development of Executive Function: Working Paper 11. Available at: www.developingchild.net (accessed 06.05.12).

Neaum, S (2005) Literacy, Pedagogy and the Early Years. Unpublished thesis. University of Nottingham.

Nichols, G (2000) *The Poet Cat*. London: Bloomsbury.

Nicholson, W (2000) *The Wind Singer*. London: Egmont.

Nutbrown, C (2003) *Recognising Early Literacy Development. Assessing Children's Achievements*. London: Paul Chapman Press.

Olsen, DR (1988) See! Jumping Some oral antecedents of literacy. In Mercer, N (1988) *Language and Literacy from an Educational Perspective*. Buckingham: Open Univesity Press.

Prout, A (2005) *The Future of Childhood*. Abingdon: RoutledgeFalmer.

Purcell-Gates, V (1995) *Other People's Words. The Cycle of Low Literacy*. London: Harvard University Press.

Rosen, M (2011) *Reflections on being the Children's Laureate and Beyond*. Cited in Lockwood, M (2011) *Bringing Poetry Alive*. London: SAGE.

Rosen, M and Blake Q, (2006) Mustard, Custard, Grumble Belly and Gravy. London: Bloomsbury.

Sanches, M and Kirshenblatt-Gimblett, B (1976) *Speech Play: Research and Resources for Studying Linguistic Creativity*. Philadelphia: University of Philadelphia Press. In Crystal, D (1998) *Language Play*. London: Penguin.

Saxton, M (2010) *Child Language. Acquisition and Development*. London: SAGE.

Siraj-Blatchford, I, Sylva, K, Muttock, S, Gilden, R and Bell, D (2002) Researching Effective Pedagogy in the Early Years. Research Report RR356, DCFS. Available at: www.education.gov.uk/publications/eOrderingDownload/RR356.pdf (accessed 06.05.12).

Smidt, S (2011) *Introducing Bruner*. London: Routledge.

Snow, CE (2001) *The Centrality of Language: A Longitudinal Study of Language and Literacy Development in Low-Income Children*. London: Institute of Education, University of London.

Stanovich, K (1992) Speculations on the cause and consequences of individual differences in early reading acquisition. In Gough, P, Ehri, L and Treiman, R (eds) *Reading Acquisition*. Hillsdale NJ: Erlbaum.

Sulzby, E (1985) Children's Emergent Reading of Storybooks. A Developmental Study. *Reading Research Quarterly*, 20 (4): 458–481.

Sulzby, E Stages of emergent writing. Available at: www.wiu.edu/itlc/ws/ws1/litfound_4.php (accessed on 08.02.12).

Sulzby, E and Rockafellow, B (2001) Sulzby classification scheme instructional profiles. Available at: www.trenton.k12.nj.us/Robbins/ReadingK/Reading-Kinder-Oct-Sulzby-Date-9-2-11.pdf (accessed on 08.02.12).

Sulzby, E and Teale, WH (1991) Emergent Literacy, in Barr, R, Kamil, M, Mosenthal, P and Pearson, PD *Handbook of Reading Research*, Volume 2. New Jersey: Lawrence Earlbaum.

Sylva, K, Meluish, E, Sammons, P, Siraj-Blatchford, I, Taggart, B and Elliot, K (2003) *Effective Provision of Pre-School Education (EPPE) Project: Findings from the Pre-School Period*. Available at: http://eppe.ioe.ac.uk/eppe/eppefindings.htm (accessed 06.05.12).

Tabors, P (1997) *One Child, Two Languages: A Guide for Preschool Educators of Children Learning English as a Second Language*. Baltimore: Paul Brookes Publishing.

Tan, S (2001) *The Red Tree*. Melbourne: Lothian Children's Books.

Tan, S (2007) *The Arrival*. Melbourne: Lothian Children's Books.

Tizzard, B and Hughes, M (1984) *Young Children Learning*. Cambridge, MA: Harvard University Press.

Tomasello, M (2003) *Constructing a Language. A Usage-Based Theory of Language Acquisition*. London: Harvard University Press.

Tough, J (1976) *Listening to Children Talking*. East Grinstead: Ward Locke.

United Nations Convention on the Rights of the Child. Available at: www.unicef.org.crc (accessed 05.02.12).

Vasilyeva, M, Waterfall, H and Huttenlocher, J (2008) Emergence of syntax: commonalities and differences across children. *Developmental Science*, 11 (1): 84–97, in Saxton, M (2001) *Child Language. Acquisition and Development*. London: SAGE.

Vygotsky, LS (1978) *Mind in Society*. Cambridge, MA: Harvard University Press.

Watson, JB and Raynor, R (1920) Conditioned emotional reactions. *Journal of Experimental Psychology*, 3: 1–14.

Weikart, PS, Schweinhart, LJ and Larner, M (1987) Movement curriculum improves children's rhythmic competence. *HighScopeReSource*, 6 (1): 8–10.

Whitehead, M (2010) *Language and Literacy in the Early Years 0–7*, 4th Edition. London: SAGE.

Whybrow, I and Reeve, R (2005) *Hey I love you!* London: Pan Children's.

Wright, C and Schweinhart, LJ (1994) *Social academic and rhythmic skills of kindergarten children*. Unpublished manuscript. Ypsilanti, MI: High Scope Educational Research Foundation (see www.high-scope.org/content.asp?contentId=234 (accessed 06.05.12).

Wyse, D and Styles, M (2007) Synthetic Phonics and the Teaching of Reading: The Debate Surrounding England's Rose Review. *Literacy*, 41 (1): 35–42.

Yaden, D, Rowe, D and MacGillivray, L (2000) *Emergent Literacy. A Polyphony of Perspectives*. CIERA. Available at: www.ciera.org/library/reports/inquiry-1/1-005/1-005.html (accessed 8.2.12).

Yeats, WB (1899/2009) *The Wind Among the Roads*. Charleston, SC: Bibliolife.

Index